nelly

NELLY BRANSON

 FriesenPress

Suite 300 - 990 Fort St
Victoria, BC, V8V 3K2
Canada

www.friesenpress.com

Copyright © 2017 by Nelly Branson
First Edition — 2017

ISBN
978-1-5255-0866-0 (Hardcover)
978-1-5255-0867-7 (Paperback)
978-1-5255-0868-4 (eBook)

1. BIOGRAPHY & AUTOBIOGRAPHY, PERSONAL MEMOIRS

Distributed to the trade by The Ingram Book Company

To the one who saved us both...
you know who you are!

The events of this book are accurate
but names, places, dates and details
have been altered.

CHAPTER 1

1983

As I prepared and wrapped Joanne's remains for the morgue, I could feel her spirit there with me in the sunlit, antiseptic hospital room. Not always did I feel the recently departed, but this time I knew she was there with me. I took extra care with the body, since she was near. Moments earlier, Joanne's husband and her two small children, ages seven and nine, had said goodbye and watched their wife and mother take her last, labored breath on earth.

A familiar voice, low and soft, asked me, "Are you okay?"

I turned to see Dr. Joe standing a couple of yards away, his intelligent, hazel eyes observing every move I made. He was a third-year medical resident I had met a few months earlier when he'd consulted on Joanne's case. He was keenly aware that his patient and I were close. He came by to check on Joanne often toward the end. Maybe on me too.

"I'm okay," I said. "This is a hard one. Those poor kids without a mother now."

"I know, and poor Ben having to raise them on his own." Shifting focus, Joe said, "Do you feel like going out tonight? I'll be leaving Eau

Claire in a week to head back to school. You look like you could use a drink. I'll buy."

I knew saying yes would be a mistake. "Yeah, okay," I said.

After the evening shift we drove down to Water Street, where the college night life was just starting to come alive—a warm summer night, music playing, and the *thump-thump* of bass spewing forth from the mouth of open bars as we strolled by. At the corner of 5th Avenue and Water Street, we found a small, secluded table in the outside courtyard of Cameraderie. The trees in the courtyard were sprinkled with Christmas lights, and the smell of grilled meat drew us in like flies to a bug zapper. Cameraderie was a quaint, pub-like bar—more upscale than the beer- soaked hole-in-the-wall college bars lining each side of Water Street. I should know … I spent many nights in all of them.

I took my first drink of the red wine Joe brought back to the table and could feel the familiar warmth as the liquor began coursing through my veins. I started to relax, and the haunting emotions of the day retreated to that place I bury deep.

Joe took my hand and looked at me with those hazel eyes, a bright smile slowly taking shape. About my height at five feet six and with dark, curly hair, Joe, a youthful looking man, had become a friend in the short time I'd known him. Tonight, I knew we would become lovers. The dance of seduction had been building for some time, and I knew tonight more than ever I needed to feel alive and loved. He knew it too.

I was slowly becoming detached from my boyfriend of three years, Michael. Ours had been a relationship built on strong desire and fun times. The chaotic ups and downs of our dating life were finally taking its toll, and although I loved Michael, it was time to let go and move on. He was not a man who was able to be there for me on an emotional level, and I was the sort with deep emotional needs.

Joe and I had a fun night and walked hand in hand the few blocks back to my apartment on Niagara Street. The night air bathed my skin as we walked along, and I was feeling warm and slightly buzzed from earlier drinks. Climbing the stairs to the second story apartment seemed to take forever as the flirtatious "dance" continued.

Inside my homey, vanilla-scented apartment we took our shoes off and snuggled on the brown plaid couch, having another drink and talking freely. Finally, Joe took my hand without a word and led me to my bedroom. The lamp from the living room cast a muted glow in the bedroom, similar to candlelight. We slowly stripped off our clothes and came together on my blue antique bed. Making love was just as slow, and he seemed to know I needed to take my time. As a wound heals in time with a Band-Aid, this lovemaking session was healing an emotional wound and needed time as well.

My apartment phone began ringing like the quarter chimes on my old grandfather clock. I knew it was Michael. He had probably driven by, spotted the living room light on, and concluded that I was home. I was determined not to answer the phone, but instead remain in the healing moment with Joe. We drifted off to the humming of the occasional ringtone. At one point, time unknown, I heard the splintering of wood, like the crack of dry thunder in the night. Then I heard heavy footsteps on the staircase, and I became clear-headed and awake within seconds.

"Get under the bed," I said to Joe. "I think Michael is coming!"

"Holy shit! You're kidding me, right?" Joe launched out of bed, grabbing his clothes and struggled to dress.

"Just hurry," I said.

I threw on my bathrobe and ran to the stair landing to see Michael ascending. His chiseled face was set hard.

"Why aren't you answering the phone?"

"I was trying to sleep. Work was bad. I didn't feel like talking," I said.

He pushed his way into the living room, and as he did I could smell the yeasty hops on his breath. He stopped mid-stride, looked toward the floor, and saw two sets of shoes, as well as matching drink glasses on the coffee table. Without saying a word, he turned and went into the bedroom as I yelled, "Michael, no!"

Michael reached under the bed, pulled Joe by his shirt collar, and hauled back and punched him in the face. I heard the crack of cartilage as Joe's nose broke. A small stream of red began trickling down his face. I let out a blood curdling scream and tried to jump between them. Joe was fully engaged in fight or flight mode and began defending himself, telling me to call 911. I'll never forget the look of complete horror on Joe's face. It clearly communicated, "What the hell did I get myself into here? I'm going to get killed!" I tried to pull Michael off and ended up getting hit myself by flailing fists. All I could do was scream, "Stop it! Stop it now!" Furniture splintered, and fists continued to fly.

It seemed as if everything was moving in slow motion. I don't know if the fight lasted one minute or ten. Suddenly, two police officers were in my bedroom breaking up the brawl. I felt as if I were in a TV drama—this couldn't be happening in real life. My beautiful light blue, serene bedroom had become the scene of a fight, and my white, frilly bedspread from my childhood was now stained with droplets of blood. I felt violated.

Thank goodness the officers appeared. One dragged Michael down the stairs by the scruff of his neck, while the other stayed with Joe and me. Statements were taken, and Michael was hauled off to spend the night in jail. I apologized to Joe, but he just looked at me with disgust and resignation as he held a towel to his bloody nose. He then walked out of my life ... for good.

Michael and his dad came to fix my broken door the next day while I was at work. It was like nothing had happened the previous night. Damage that magically gets erased.

Several months passed, and I was feeling emotionally strong. One day, a phone call out of nowhere came as a shock.

"I have to see you," Michael said. Something in his voice—sadness and possibly regret— made me drive over to his apartment. Perhaps I was hoping for closure to this chapter of my life.

Nelly

Michael answered the door with tears streaming down his face. His hand reached out to mine. My heart leapt out of my chest and landed directly in his palm. He professed his love for me and explained his jealous rage. The only time I ever saw him cry was that day, and not a day since ... even through his father's funeral, the death of his best friend, the loss of his child, and every other tragedy. Not a tear has been spent. How would I know? I married him. Glinda told me to, so I did.

CHAPTER 2
MOMMY DEAREST

There is nothing as strong as the mother and child bond. I was placed into my mother's arms on July 25, 1959. My mother, Georgia, gazed into my green eyes and told me that I would be hers forever. She meant it. Although the umbilical cord had been severed shortly after the birth process, in reality it would remain invisibly in place for another four decades.

I was born at Luther Hospital in Eau Claire, WI. The circle of life would lead me back to this particular Midwest town and this particular hospital as well. They both became an integral part of my life. Here I went to college, met my husband, got married, and started my career. I get ahead of myself, though. Back to the beginning.

The first time in my life I should have died was a month before my birth. My mother, eight months pregnant, was sitting at a large picture window in my paternal grandparents' old white farmhouse. It was one of those unusually warm, humid June days—one that felt like you were sitting in a sauna. The moisture clung to the air like spiders to a web.

Alone in the house, my mother was seated at the secretary desk, penning a note to her parents. She gazed outside at a giant canopied elm tree in the front yard. Earlier there had been a marked breeze, but now the newly blossomed leaves were as still as lily pads in a marsh. Nothing was moving outside, and the sky had quickly become a threatening mottled grey. Instinct told my mother to quickly seek shelter.

As she descended into the basement, the wind whipped up like someone had ordered the switch of a fan turned on. When she reached the underground safety of the old blocked limestone walls, she heard a tremendous crash and felt the farmhouse vibrate.

The storm abated as quickly as it had started. My mother ascended out of the steep, musty hole and looked toward where she had been sitting. A large arm of the elm tree had crashed through the roof, landing on the chair that we, as one, had occupied. All that remained were splinters of wood that looked like the lifeless legs of the Wicked Witch of the East peeking out of the fallen house in Oz. That was the first time my mother saved my life. There would be more.

I was brought up during a time when pop culture aired shows on television in black and white. A show like *Father Knows Best*, or one in which Donna Reed, who was "America's favorite mom," came bounding down the stairs in a starched plaid dress, eagerly ready for another hard day on the home front doing mundane chores like laundry, ironing, and cleaning. It was a time before Neil Armstrong took his first steps on the moon, and before Ed Sullivan introduced to the United States the fab four known as the Beatles. I was born four years before the nation's devastating loss of President John F. Kennedy … the assassination transitioning America's hope for the future to the death of Camelot. It was a simpler time, but not necessarily a better one.

I came across an internet blog post; Larry Temple, "The Good Wife's Guide" from Housekeeping Monthly, May 13th, 1955. https://larrytemple.wordpress.com/2008/05/01/actual-1955-good-housekeeping-article/ . I don't know if this article is authentic, but it gives a sense of the role expectations in the 1950s and 1960s. Here is an excerpt from that blog addressed to wives of that time:

+ Have dinner ready. Plan ahead, even the night before, to have a delicious meal ready on time for his return. This is a way of letting him know that you have been thinking about him and are concerned about his needs. Most men are hungry when they come home, and the prospect of a good meal (especially his favorite dish) is part of the warm welcome needed.

+ Prepare yourself. Take fifteen minutes to rest so you'll be refreshed when he arrives. Touch up your make-up, put a ribbon in your hair, and be fresh-looking. He has just been with a lot of work-weary people.

+ Be a little gay and a little more interesting for him. His boring day may need a lift, and one of your duties is to provide it.

+ Clear away the clutter. Make one last trip through the main part of the house just before your husband arrives. Run a dust cloth over the tables.

+ Over the cooler months of the year, you should prepare and light a fire for him to unwind by. Your husband will feel he has reached a haven of rest and order, and it will give you a lift too. After all, catering for his comfort will provide you with immense personal satisfaction.

+ Minimize all noise. At the time of his arrival, eliminate all noise of the washer, dryer, or vacuum. Encourage the children to be quiet.

+ Be happy to see him.

+ Greet him with a warm smile and show sincerity in your desire to please him.

+ Listen to him. You may have a dozen important things to tell him, but the moment of his arrival is not the time. Let him talk first—remember, his topics of conversation are more important than yours.

+ Make the evening his. Never complain if he comes home late or goes out to dinner or other places of entertainment without you. Instead, try to understand his world of strain and pressure and his very real need to be at home and relax.

+ Your goal: To try and make sure your home is a place of peace, order, and tranquility where your husband can renew himself in body and spirit.
+ Don't greet him with complaints and problems.
+ Make him comfortable. Have him lean back in a comfortable chair or have him lie down in the bedroom. Have a cool or warm drink ready for him.
+ Arrange his pillow and offer to take off his shoes. Speak in a low, soothing, and pleasant voice.
+ Don't ask him questions about his actions or question his judgment or integrity. Remember, he is the master of the house and as such will always exercise his will with fairness and truthfulness. You have no right to question him. A good wife always knows her place.

Can you imagine the current generation reading this? I can see the OMG, WTF, LMAO responses. However, those were the spousal dynamics of the era into which I was born. My mother, Georgia, took this guide to heart. Especially the last bullet point—as I would find out in years to come.

Shortly after my birth, I began to cause problems. Causing problems became my mantra in life, intentional or not. At this particular time, I developed an umbilical hernia. An umbilical hernia is a bulging in the abdominal wall around the belly button. I must have been four weeks old when they decided the hernia was too large and needed to be surgically reduced and closed.

My mom said I morphed from an angel baby before surgery to Rosemary's Baby after surgery. I was a horror to care for, and she became exhausted. I smelled like ether, which was the anesthetic they used in the late 1950s. Some people say if you've smelled a dead body, you never forget that odor. Well, I guess ether was the same way—a pungent, awful smell that hung around like maggots on a compost pile. The smell penetrated the body for days after surgery.

My mother would try to comfort me through the post-surgical pain, but would end up throwing up as a result of being around me. I don't think that event improved the mother and infant bonding experience. Maybe it was the beginning of the love/hate cycle of our relationship.

The surgery left a small, two-inch scar across my abdomen right above my belly button. When I was about three years old, I'd go around lifting up my dress, pointing to my scar, and saying, "Me broken ... all fixed" to anyone—strangers or not—who would listen. Little did I know that it would take another thirty plus years for that statement to be truly achieved.

Georgia was also instrumental in making sure we were connected to our extended family. Holidays, birthdays, and weekends were spent with relatives—grandparents, aunts, uncles, cousins. One sunny, hot summer day we were at my aunt and uncle's cottage on Tuttle Lake in South Central Wisconsin. I must have been about four years old at the time. The water was shimmering like diamonds on glass, and I was drawn to it like a magnet. My mother had instructed me to never go out on the dock by myself without an adult or a life jacket on. I decided this beautiful, sunny afternoon to do just that.

I went running out on the dock to see if I could spot fish swimming beneath the water's surface. As I leaned over the dock to search for the elusive pinfish and minnows, I tripped and the water swallowed me whole. This wasn't a shallow lake, so I was well above my head and couldn't swim. What happened next was mystifying.

I was floating above my body and looking at me under the water, watching tiny bubbles come out of my nose and trickle toward the surface. My green eyes were as big as saucers, and my blonde hair was gently swishing back and forth across my face in the underwater current. My limbs were moving wildly, as if trying to run in place.

Nelly

Physically, I wasn't feeling anything. It was the strangest and most peaceful experience ever. I remember not really wanting to return to that thrashing body. How long I was under water before my mother plucked me out, saving me again, I do not know. However, since that early experience, I have never been afraid of death. It isn't that I care to die—I'm just not afraid of it, unlike most people. I was told that summer day that it wasn't my time.

My parents were in their early twenties when they had my sister and me. Susie was two years older than me, and we had a close little family. My parents, being young and social, would throw parties every few months in the half-finished basement of our house. The room was decked out with orange and green shag carpeting, bubble and lava lamps, and a long wooden hi-fi system that looked like a brown coffin and held the turntable where favorite records were played. Frank Sinatra, Elvis Presley, Buddy Holly, Billy Holiday, and Bing Crosby's voices would float through the house on party night, as would laughter. My parents seemed really happy in those early years.

The day after a party there would be the smell of food, stale beer, and cigarette smoke lingering in the house … like the smell of a rural carnival. Ceramic ashtrays full of half-smoked cigarette butts were positioned like decorations on the end tables. Half-filled and empty brown Old Milwaukee beer bottles would be scattered around, some upright, others lying nestled in the shag carpet. It was like finding a big, brown turd in the middle of a pumpkin patch. The adults had all the fun and the kids did all the tidying up work. I wanted to be the adult having the fun. I hated the filth of clean up days.

My dad began his career as a guidance counselor, became principal, and finally superintendent of schools. The party-goers tended to be fellow teachers in those early days. One of the teachers remains with me to this day. His name is Jeffry.

CHAPTER 3

JEFFRY

Most people when they are alone ... are alone. Not me. During my young adult years whenever I closed my eyes, a fuzzy image of Jeffry was there. Jeffry had dark hair and piercing blue eyes. A friendly face most of the time. My dad's hunting, fishing, and work buddy. Someone who was constantly around our house.

At times in my youth, especially when I became anxious, Jeffry's face became well-defined. Like when you go to the ophthalmologist's office and those round glass disks click into the machine you are looking through. An image goes from hazy to distinct. That's how it was periodically with Jeffry's image ... as if the glass had clicked into place and his face was clear-cut. He has been living with me since the night of one of my parents' parties.

As this particular party was in full swing, the time came for my sister and me to go to bed. My mother must have been busy entertaining, because she delegated her duty of the nighttime tucking in not to my dad, but to their friend, Jeffry.

After saying prayers, Jeffry cocooned me **into** my fluffy twin bed, his face inches from mine. He didn't kiss my cheek as friends do to say goodnight; instead, he kissed me on my lips... and there he lingered.

nelly

His warm fingers grazed my face as he told me I was beautiful. He shushed me, whispering to be a good girl.

As a child, you don't really know what's happening ... just that it's not supposed to happen. Why was this grown man, a friend, touching my child's body in such a way? As the intimate violation intensified, I stared at the crack across my bedroom ceiling, an analogy of what was happening to my soul. That night amongst the pink and glitter, and the stoic faces of stuffed animals, the innocence of a small child was lost. Since that night, Jeffry lives with me in a locked compartment in my brain, never to have the key unlatch the hasp.

There is a poem called "The Man in The Glass," published in 1934 by Peter "Dale" Winbrow Sr. The author talks about looking at himself in a mirror. The intent of the poem is to be true to oneself, to the person who looks back at you from the mirror. However, one lyric of the poem reminds me of Jeffry, who continues to this day to be my "man in the glass."

He's the fellow to please, never mind all the rest
For he's with you clear up to the end
And you've passed the most dangerous, difficult test
If the man in the glass is your friend

I passed the difficult test, but the man in the glass is not my friend. I cannot escape Jeffry. He is with me until the end. My mother fed me to the devil. This time, she was not there to save me.

Jeffry was like a tornado. He came, did his damage, and disappeared. The abuse did not linger, but the damage lasted a lifetime. My guess is he moved on to other victims after leaving me alone.

Later in life, during my father's memorial service, I saw Jeffry again. He looked nothing like the man in the glass that lives with me. After the service, he departed from the church sanctuary with a slow gait while using a walker. He stopped in front of me, and his limbs were constantly trembling due to whatever medical affliction he suffered from. His face and hands were covered with wart-like blemishes of all sizes. I guess he grew into looking like the monster he was. Karma can be a bitch!

Jeffry had the same blue eyes, but they were now rheumy with age. As I looked through the blue windows into the soul of the devil, I saw a brief glimmer of sadness and sorrow. Since his speech was affected by his medical condition, he said three words to me very slowly in a shaky timbre: "I ... am ... sorry." I hesitated slightly before replying, "Thank you." I turned abruptly on my heels and didn't look back.

I do not know if his words were meant as a condolence for the loss of my father or an apology for the trauma he caused years before. I chose to believe the latter of the two. I forgave him, closed that chapter of my life, and threw away the key for good.

CHAPTER 4

SECOND GRADE

The longest road traveled at the age of seven was from the back of the airless second grade classroom to the front. As I passed the old wooden desks aligned like cemetery tombstones, I felt the bile rising, burning in the back of my throat. Although the color red was in my wheelhouse, I was ashamed to be wearing the crimson blanket across my face as I neared the front.

A few moments earlier, my father had been discussing something with my teacher, Ms. Erickson—a woman who could enter the hot, dank classroom and turn it quickly into the frozen tundra with a mere glance. After a hushed discussion with my teacher, my father pivoted on his black wingtip shoes. He strode out the door with his suit-tail flapping like crisp linens hung out to dry in the summer breeze. He did not glance my way. That is when the butterflies descended on my stomach like the army of flying monkeys did to Dorothy in *The Wizard of Oz*. I knew I was in trouble again.

It had been a rocky year. For some reason, this short, matronly teacher with a beehive hairdo and glasses circling the end of her nose did not like me. Perhaps she was expecting me to be like my nice, quiet, studious sister, Susie. Not happening. God willing, my baby sister, who was born that year, would be a bright light for the world and follow in Susie's footsteps.

Throughout the year, most of my classmates would hover over their assigned papers like buzzards with a fresh kill, concentrating on writing their answers. As they were diligently working away, I'd gaze out the encased windows to the adjacent hazel hillside, wanting to escape and run free from this squared prison. At the appropriate time, my internal clock would ring me back to the task at hand. Before handing my paper to the pigtailed girl in front of me, I would place a huge X across my entire paper and then sign my name "Nelly Anderson!" Exclamation mark included.

When I wasn't being distracted by school-day events, I tried to be productive … only my idea of being productive was writing henscratched love notes about the boys in class. My desk overflowed with proclamations of love. I was particularly interested in Stevie, the blue-eyed, shaggy-haired wonder whom I chased relentlessly on the school playground at recess. My best friend was Danny… a dark haired, serious, nerdy kid hiding behind thick square glasses. I found the girls in my class to be giggly and inane, so I chose to play with the boys. If there was a ball involved at recess, I would be there. It didn't matter if it was a dodgeball, baseball, or football—it called my name. It would be the boys and me. Occasionally another girl would want "in," but they couldn't keep up with the boys like I could, and they quickly fell to the wayside.

Danny wasn't really athletic, but since kindergarten he had been my best buddy. Although his young personality was already the broody professor type, he was my number one pal, and I enjoyed his quirky ways. In return for my friendship, he always had my back—literally, as he sat behind me in class. When I'd get dragged to the bathroom by Ms. Erickson for a soap-mouth-washing, he would be there to help dry my angry tears and soothe my ruffled ego. If I was being inattentive and was called upon by Ms. Erickson to answer a moronic question of hers, Danny would quickly whisper the answer in my ear.

nelly

During one class field trip, Danny and I were sitting together on the bus, chatting away like a couple of long lost girlfriends. As we grew weary from the day's activities, Danny put his arm around me, and we both drifted into a contented round of silence, eyes closed. Ms. Erickson came swooping down on the two of us like an eagle clawing its dinner from the surface of a serene lake. Apparently having an arm around me was not appropriate behavior for a seven-year-old. Danny untangled his arm from my dampened neck and we resumed our idle conversation. When Ms. Erickson returned to her seat at the front of the bus, I smiled and grabbed Danny's hand and held on tight. Tethered souls.

As I now made my way toward the front of the class, bile rising, butterflies dancing in the center of my being, I knew my father's visit was caustic. Classmates tittered, and girls smothered their giggles as my face radiated fire, and my ears started ringing. Even though I wanted to run out the door and down the hall to the embrace of my father's office, I knew it was no safe haven. So I marched to the outstretched arm of my teacher. Her claw-like hand opened slowly, as would a clam proudly baring a beautiful pearl. Only no pearl was hidden … only a familiar hen-scratched note, declaring as only a seven-year-old can, her undying love for a boy named Stevie.

At her direction, I read my private, innermost feelings in front of the class. Laughter rang out from my peers. I shriveled. As I stumbled to my seat, the biggest cruelty of all assaulted my senses—my Danny, pointing, laughing, and joining in with the mockery. I felt like Hester Prynne as I hung my head and stared at the cracked wooden floor. Another fissure, similar to the fracture in the floor, adorned my psyche. Retreating to the sanctuary of my home that night, I found out the stark reality of my father's school day visit. My baby sister was dead.

17

CHAPTER 5

BABY SISTER

From a child's stance, I look up into my mother's face. There were tears streaming down her upper body like a gentle rainfall. They landed on the front of her blouse and mixed with the lactation droplets already there. The life force that was meant as nutrition for my baby sister was dripping from my mother's breasts onto her shirt. The salty tears signifying my sister's death were the more prominent body fluid seen there.

The circle of life was right before my eyes. It displayed like a grand plan on my mother's upper garment. The pain I felt for my mother in that instant and the loss I felt for my sister was enormous.

She lived exactly four months to the day, struggling every day since birth to survive, despite her congenital heart defect. She was born with a small hole in her heart. In death, her heart was healed. In life, the hole transferred to our hearts.

I wasn't allowed to attend my sister's funeral. I saw pictures of her small, white casket adorned with white lilies. Weeks later, I begged to be taken to her gravesite. On top of a small mound of freshly moved earth was a mauve gravestone the size of a dessert pan. The polished top showed a black outline of an angel—my baby sister. The circle of life again etched in dark print: March 11, 1966–July 11, 1966.

We donated a picture to our church in my sister's name. I can still see the painting—the outstretched hands of Jesus surrounded by five cherubic children sitting at His feet, staring lovingly into His face. Every Sunday when I walked by that picture, I wondered which child was my sister. We never spoke of her in our house again. It was as if she'd never existed.

CHAPTER 6

FOUNDATION

Years ago, there was a book: Robert Fulghum, *All I Really Need to Know I Learned in Kindergarten* New York: Villard Books, 1988. 196 pages. Fulghum alludes to lessons learned in kindergarten and applies those basic lessons to adulthood: Some of the rules listed in his book are:

+ Share everything.
+ Play fair.
+ Don't hit people.
+ Say you are sorry when you hurt someone.
+ Clean up your own mess.

I could rewrite that book and entitle mine *All I Really Need to Know I Learned from My Family.* The lessons I learned were:

+ If someone behaves inappropriately, pretend it never happened.
+ Bury emotions; do not attempt to communicate them.
+ Be sneaky—it pays off.
+ No matter what happens, act like everything is fine.
+ When in emotional pain, drink alcohol.

Having an IQ close to 135, I was a quick study. I learned those lessons well.

nelly

At the time of my sister's death, we were living in a small town of about 3,000 people in southern Wisconsin. We had a new house in a brand-new subdivision. My parents' bedroom was on one end of the house, and my sister's and mine on the other end. In the middle of the house was the third bedroom. The crib was quickly dismantled. This room became the catch-all. Instead of a nursery, the ironing board with water spritzer was set up. There was a small couch where my sister or I were exiled to recuperate if one of us became ill. We had a little round wooden table where red ABCs were prominently displayed in the wood grain. I spent many days as a young child coloring or drawing at this table, my mother ironing or my sister reading on the couch beside me.

My mother's ability to ignore or deny loss, abuse and dysfunction in the home had a lifelong impact on our relationship.

I've always enjoyed watching investigative shows and trying to figure out the "whodunits." One thing I learned by watching these programs is that often investigators will have child victims draw as a way to communicate what happened to them. In the Jeffry era, I tried to do the same. I remember drawing pictures of our family or friends. I would draw men with prominent pant zippers, or stick men with giant penises.

I don't know if it was a developmental phase I was going through, or if it was my way of trying to communicate what had happened to me. My guess is I was trying to draw attention to what had occurred to me with the only medium that was available to me as a small child. If I had a daughter who started to draw male genitals, I would probably investigate why she was doing that.

Not Georgia. I got reprimanded every time I drew a picture. I was told I was being inappropriate. My attempt at communication was equivalent to having a door slammed in my face. Remember, my mother had the job of keeping the house peaceful and serene. Even if she ever suspected anything was wrong, a word was never mentioned.

For all her faults, my mother tried to be a good mother, and she worked hard at being the "good wife." She took her role seriously, as any spouse and mother did in the '60s and '70s. Her job was to take care of the children and house. My dad supported us financially.

My mother's office was mainly the kitchen; my father's, a few blocks away at school. I never remember my father involved in physically taking care of us, except one time when my mom had to have some minor "female" surgery. His job was to make fried fish for dinner. The only other domesticated role he had was to make us popcorn on Sunday nights. We would settle in with buttery goodness while watching the *Sonny and Cher* or *Carol Burnett* shows. In our house, Sunday nights were declared "family night," and God forbid anything get in the way of us bonding while watching TV and munching on popped corn.

For the most part, my childhood was normal, but interspersed with insanity. It was the dichotomy of my existence. All I really ever knew. I believe most parents love their children unconditionally and try their best to do the right thing in raising them. I believe most kids love their parents the same way. I did, anyway. Susie, on the other hand, never liked our father.

I'm not sure why I thought my dad needed a son. I guess as a child I presumed all men wanted sons, and all women wanted daughters. Anyway, I grew up trying to be the son my dad never had. Susie wouldn't have anything to do with our father. I would be his shadow, right there next to him if he needed an extra pair of hands fixing something around the house. I grew up knowing what a Phillips screwdriver was and what an Allen wrench looked like, and what a Sawzall was and how to handle a drill press or table saw. I would play baseball, football, or mow the yard. I was my dad's substitute son.

I was also his staunchest fishing buddy. There was nothing I liked better than being at our cottage on White Potato Lake. Serenity for me was a calm summer night in an old row boat catching perch with a worm and bobber and watching the sun crawl along the sky until it disappeared. We would sneak frozen Milky Way bars to snack on and fish well after dinner until the day's end. Those were good times with my dad.

My father was a handsome man, very quiet, mild-mannered, and methodical in his approach to life. He was of average height with a small beer belly. I thought he was the best dad ever. I was proud to be his daughter.

Growing up as the daughter of the superintendent of schools had some drawbacks. We always had to dress nicely, go to church every Sunday, be polite, act maturely, and achieve scholastically. We were poised as the example for other families as the "best of the best." Even our friends were hand-picked from the "preacher and teacher" kiddie pool. Expectations and standards in our household were very high.

School teachers either hated my sister and me or loved us, depending on how they felt about our father. Usually it was also dependent upon how well contract negotiations for the school year went.

Being the superintendent's daughter also had its perks. Since my dad was the one to call off school on snow days, our family would be the first to know. My sister and I were allowed to sleep in if my dad called off school. I was impressed with the power he held.

Sometimes on Sunday afternoons my dad would take the school keys and open the gym for us. We'd get to drink all the chocolate milk we wanted and play on the climbing rope, trampoline, and other gym equipment. Everyone in the community knew who we were, and everywhere we went our entire family was held in high esteem.

Most parents with two or more children say that each child is very different. My sister Susie and I fit that scenario. Being two years apart we were close in age, but we couldn't have been more different in personality.

Both of us had blonde hair. Susie had blue eyes, and mine were green. Susie was the studious type who liked to sit in her room and read books or listen to music. When fully grown, she stood at five-feet-six-inches and was heavier set than me. She inherited the German side of the family's build—a big bosom and larger behind.

I liked to be out and about in the world, playing, being around friends, and constantly moving or active. Although the same height as my sister, I was leaner and athletic with a nicely proportioned shape. My build was inherited from our Norwegian ancestry.

When we were young, my mother liked to dress the two of us in a matched fashion. I think she expected us to be similar, even though we weren't. She tried very hard to keep everything equal and balanced between us—the same clothes, the same number of presents, the same dolls, and so on.

We were around age six and eight when we got our tonsils out together. We were even in the same hospital room. The beds were not positioned next to each other, but across the room from one another. They probably were positioned that way so we could see each other when the head of the bed was slightly raised. Maybe that was meant to comfort us. I didn't like being in the hospital or away from home. Susie didn't seem to mind either situation.

I remember one night after surgery ringing the call button for the nurse. Those poor nurses ... I was on the bell constantly. I was home-sick, feeling better, sick of popsicles, and wanting to leave. The nurses, finally fed up with my continued annoyance, gave me a rectal sup-pository to knock me out for the night and make me groggy into the next day. The following morning, the doctor made his rounds. After examining my sister and me, he made the comment to my parents that when our energy levels showed signs of improvement, we could go home.

I looked over at Susie in the bed across from me. She was sleeping, oblivious to anything around her. She had severe seasonal allergies and always had Kleenex tissues stuffed up each nostril. So while Susie lay there looking like a human tissue box with no intention of leaving the comfort of her hospital bed, I had other plans.

nelly

The doctor took my parents into the hallway to discuss our care, and by the time they came back into the room, I was fully dressed with my suitcase packed and my hospital bed made. As my feet dangled from the bed, pumping wildly, I said, "I'm ready to go home."

My comatose sister never moved a muscle or opened her eyes. The doctor, chuckling, told me I was a sneaky little kid, but it looked like I was ready to go home. My parents took me home. Being sneaky worked out well for me and got me what I wanted. The unconscious tissue box kid got left behind.

To fully understand the family into which my sister and I were born, you would need to know something about the families into which my parents were born. My father had an interesting childhood. His father worked on the railroad in Eau Claire. When my dad was ten, his father was working one night during a thunderstorm. Grandpa Bill was running across the top of the railroad cars, doing whatever it was he did for his job, and got struck by lightning. He died instantly. The pocket watch he was wearing stopped exactly at 10:02, the time of the lightning strike and his death. There was a burn hole in the top of his head and through the sole of his left foot. Rumor has it that my grandfather was quite the ladies' man and was not faithful to my grandmother. There goes that karma thing again.

My dad's mom died when I was ten. She always struck me as a depressed, kind of grumpy, old woman … although she was an excellent baker. I can't remember her ever smiling. She was about five-feet-five with the physique of a brick—large bosoms, large tummy, large butt. She was a squarely built woman, like SpongeBob SquarePants would look if all sides were equal. Her biggest concern in life was whether you ate enough fruit and vegetables and if you had a daily bowel movement. Of course, I probably wouldn't have been too happy either if my parents had named me Dorc, short for Dorcas. Maybe it was different back then, but in my day, kids would have relentlessly teased someone with the name Dorc. Maybe she was teased, and that was why she was so grumpy.

My dad was surrounded by women his whole life, and they spoiled him. Along with his mother, with whom he had a close relationship, he had a sister eleven years his senior, who was like a second mother to him, as well as his "aunties." As the story goes, they waited on him hand and foot.

My mother's side of the family was interesting as well. My mom was the youngest of three kids; she was the "oops" conceived later in my grandparents' life. She had an older sister and brother. She loved her brother dearly, but didn't particularly like her sister. She definitely did not like her father, my Grandpa John. He owned and ran a gas station, and because of the work load was never home.

There was some sort of dysfunctional relationship between my mother and her father. I never found out what the issue was; my mom would just tell me it was due to her being "strong-willed" as a child, and my grandfather being "too old" to know how to handle such a rebellious kid.

My mom's mom, my Grandmother Helga, was a wonderful woman. As I grew up, we had a close relationship. About five-feet-seven, she stood ramrod straight and was always dressed impeccably. Soft, white hair surrounded robin's egg-blue eyes.

She was an English teacher, never got her driver's license, but was fiercely independent. I'm sure she made quite a positive mark on her students' lives. There was just an aura around her of youth, energy, intelligence, kindness, love, and dignity. She was always helpful to her children and involved in her grandchildren's lives.

My grandparents lived at 2552 Atlanta Avenue, and I always thought it was so cool to have a rhyming address. I have many fond memories of visiting 2552. My grandmother's house was the hub for holidays when we were little. One time, my cousin and I locked ourselves in her bathroom downstairs and decided to take all her tubes of lipstick out of the drawer and color on the walls. After we were in the bathroom awhile working on our masterpiece, the parents tracked us down, and we refused to come out.

nelly

After finding the tool to unlock the bathroom door from the outside, they entered the small room. You should have seen the blood drain from adult faces as they looked at our "decorating." My grandmother, without missing a beat, said, "Well, that is really pretty." To my parents she said, "it's okay, it needed to be painted anyway." So much for consequences for bad behavior.

I remember one holiday get-together at my aunt and uncle's house in Bensenville, Illinois. The men of the family were sitting in the family room watching a football game, drinking beer, and smoking cigarettes. There was the haze of smoke, the game announcer's excited voice calling out the play by play action of the athletes, and the occasional chuckle, retort, or comment made by a male relative.

I'd become bored with my cousin's games and wanted to hang out with the men and watch the football game. My grandfather told me to stay where I was and not set foot in the room. They didn't want me in there. Trying to be an obedient child, I placed my hands on each side of the door jamb leading into the family room. Then I made the tragic mistake of leaning forward with my body into the family room, straining to see the game while still hanging onto the door jamb. Technically speaking, I hadn't set foot in the room.

Well, I must have crossed an invisible boundary. No sooner had I begun to suspend like the leaning tower of Pisa when my grandfather leapt out of his chair and came toward me, yelling, "I told you to stay out of here." He grabbed me and walloped my butt hard while throwing me across my aunt's linoleum kitchen floor. I was skidding at such a fast rate across the floor that the only thing that could stop me was the kitchen cupboard. I was hoping to be like the cartoon Road Runner who would stop on a dime just short of slamming into a cliff. Only I kept going and hit the cliff.

After the cupboard stopped me, I began to cry. I think I was more shocked than anything. I cried not only because I was physically hurt, but emotionally I couldn't understand why my grandfather did that to me. I thought I was following the rules.

My mother came to my rescue immediately and began screaming at her father. Then she completely broke down crying and rushed me to the nearest restroom. She locked the door, and the two of us just hugged each other and cried. My mom kept telling me it wasn't my fault—it was hers. She told me that her father didn't like her, so he took his anger out on me. I don't think my little brain really understood that logic. I remember thinking to myself, *If Grandpa doesn't like you, I get hit?* Somehow that didn't really seem fair.

After my mom was sure I had settled down and was okay, we left the security of the bathroom. My mother then mixed a strong alcoholic drink and continued to down it like it was a glass of milk. The incident wasn't talked about, and nothing more was said to my grandfather. Everyone carried on like nothing happened. My dad continued to watch the football game, uninterrupted.

The lessons learned from my family during these early years, as well as family genetics laid the foundation for my future uncontrolled and dysfunctional behavior. I wasn't able to comprehend Fulghum's Kindergarten lesson's until well into middle age.

CHAPTER 7

THIRTEEN

Twenty-six steps. Each step loomed before me like a mile while running a marathon. Up five steps from the garage, a sharp left turn, another three through the den. Five more steps through the dining room, eight around the kitchen table into the hallway and another five until I hit my bedroom door.

At the base of the garage steps I lowered my head and rested my forehead in the crook of my left arm. "Please, Lord, let me make it this last little bit," I prayed. I gathered strength, concentrating hard on putting one foot in front of the other. It was a miracle I had made it this far.

As I made my way through the house, the only audible noise was the scraping of a pan— a dull *thunk* of a wooden spoon hitting metal. I got to the kitchen and saw my angel food birthday cake sitting to the left of the stove, fresh out of the oven. The slight scent of vanilla was in the air, and the brown crust peeked out from the aluminum pan like a ruffle on a dress. The cake was resting upside down, the middle of it swallowing the neck of a brown beer bottle. My mother turned from the stove.

"How was the bike ride?" she asked.

Head bent, not looking her in the eyes, I quietly replied. "We rode all afternoon; I don't feel well. I'm going to lie down for a while."

"Okay, get some rest; dinner will be ready in about an hour."

"K," I answered.

I lumbered to my room, where a sea of blue hit me and enveloped me in a calm embrace. I dove into my bed and felt the familiar comfort surround me. I said a quick thank you to The Man Upstairs and didn't wake up again until the next night. I missed my thirteenth birthday celebration. Happy birthday to me!

While most of my appointed preacher-and-teacher-family friends were having sleepovers, skating parties, picnics, and family parties for their thirteenth birthdays, I ended up getting drunk. Dangerously drunk. Christening what would become turbulent teenage years.

By this time we were living in a medium-size northern Wisconsin town. The town was known primarily for shipbuilding and the paper industry. Nestled on the western side of the bay of Green Bay, across from Door County, it was a quaint and historic little town.

My father's career continued to progress. He was busy with board meetings, referendums, and plans to build new schools to better the community's educational system. The family was settled into a comfortable normal routine. Then, as hormones started to surface, I turned thirteen.

Out in the driveway, on our quiet street, I was shooting hoops in my cut-off jean shorts, one of my many homemade halter tops, and my black and white boys' tennis shoes. It was a beautiful summer day. There wasn't a cloud in the sky, and there was only a slight, warm breeze coming from the bay. The flowers were all in bloom. The heavy smell of dampness touched with decaying fish was in the air. We lived a few blocks from a private yacht club and beach. You could hear the seagulls squawking in glee in the distance as they circled the bay looking for their next meal.

I was playing the basketball game H.O.R.S.E. by myself. If I made a difficult shot, I would have to repeat it. If I missed on the second shot, I would get a letter until H-O-R-S-E was spelled out and the game was done. The game was usually played with another person. Whoever spelled H.O.R.S.E. last was the winner. The only contenders in sight were the old folks across the street that lived in a nursing home complex. I didn't think one of the grey-haired men or women with walkers strolling the flower-clad grounds would be interested in a game of H.O.R.S.E., so I continued on by myself.

As the orange-striped ball cleared the rim and went through the netted hoop with a *whoosh*, I saw a couple of kids on bicycles turning the corner of Shore Drive, heading my way. As they came closer, I could see they were wearing swimsuits underneath their cut-off jeans and T-shirts. Their stripped beach towels were coiled up like snakes in their front bike baskets.

The girls' names were Julie and Gail. They lived in the neighborhood and were in my grade at school. If you looked at the grades of kids in my class on a normal distribution of a bell curve, I would fall into the upper 2.5 percent of the bell curve, and Julie and Gail would be in the bottom 2.5 percent. They were not stellar students.

Gail gave off the New Age vibe. She was tall with a nicely proportioned figure, a severe case of acne, and a high forehead. She always wore her long, brown hair in a braid past her butt to mid-thigh. I could easily picture her as an adult meditating with incense burning, or smoking pot behind beaded doorways, with New Age music in the background. She was generally quiet and soft spoken—not the sharpest tack in the box.

Then there was Julie. She was short with an athletic figure and reddish brown hair cut to her shoulders. She was the type of person you instantly knew had entered a room, even without looking. She had a presence about her … an aura that was extremely strong. Not to mention she was Italian and audibly loud. If you didn't sense her presence, you would hear it. I could picture Julie married to someone like Henry Winkler's "The Fonz," riding a Harley motorcycle, and wearing leather chaps with a cigarette dangling from her lips. She was a rough-around-the-edges type character. Here they were, Mutt and Jeff of the female persuasion, approaching my house.

My eyes were fixated on Julie as she approached A memory was still fresh in my mind of an experience we'd shared that past school year. I'd been sitting in math class and Julie was staring at me from a couple of seats away. I could feel the intensity of the glare, and I got the feeling she was trying to size me up. It was as if she was looking at me as some "goody-two-shoes." I think she was trying to figure out how she might manipulate me over to the dark side of life.

I was the favorite student in this math class. My teacher was always praising my abilities in front of the other kids. Even though I acted like it was embarrassing, I secretly loved both the male and academic attention from my teacher.

After class while I was in the hallway heading to English, Julie approached me and said, "I have the answers to the history test tomorrow. Do you want them?"

Trying to fit in with the rougher crowd, I said nonchalantly, "Sure, why not!"

Julie quickly glanced around and then handed me a sheet of paper. Giving it a cursory scan, I saw numbers on the sheet from one to one hundred with capital letters next to each number—A, C, D, C, B, A, and so on. I thought Julie was initially bluffing, but here in front of me appeared to be the entire answer key to the upcoming history test.

I quickly folded up the paper and stashed it between the books I was carrying. It felt to me like every kid in the hallway had just witnessed the crime of the century. I'm sure my face looked shocked as well as guilty. I slunk down the hallway to my next class with a false smile glued on my face, looking and feeling like the Cheshire Cat.

I went home that night and memorized the list Julie had given me. The next day we took the history exam, and it seemed as though the answer key I had memorized fit well with the test questions. Without reading further than the first five questions, I wrote down the memorized answers, finished the test within minutes, handed in my paper, and got a 100 percent on the exam.

The following week I began feeling guilt-ridden. One morning I couldn't take it anymore. I rose from my seat, went up to the student intern teacher seated at his battered desk, and said, "I cheated on last week's test." The student teacher looked at me with a very perplexed expression. I leaned down into his ear and with a shaky voice stated, "I had all the answers ahead of time for the test last week."

He didn't say a word, but he kept staring at me like I had two heads, or had just told him Santa Claus was real. When it finally sunk in what I was saying, he quickly rose, said "excuse me" to the class, and hurriedly exited the classroom, the door slamming shut in his wake.

Shortly thereafter I was summoned to my dad's office, where I was interrogated and had to confess the series of events leading up to my crime. I got an F for the quarter in history. I wasn't praised for doing the right thing by telling the truth of my misdeed; instead, I was scolded for cheating and received a B average for the semester in history. In my family, receiving anything lower than an "A" was considered a failure. In my eyes, that meant I was a failure as well.

The ironic thing about the whole experience was that I would have gotten close to that 100 percent on my own with as much effort as it took to memorize the cheat sheet. I committed a crime to prove I wasn't such a "goody-two-shoes." The next time I saw Julie; she laughed the situation off and said she'd ended up with an F as well. It didn't bother her in the least.

That experience behind us, I got a sinking feeling in the pit of my stomach as I watched the spoked wheels of the bikes turning into my driveway.

"What are you up to?" Julie asked.

"Not much; just shooting some baskets," I replied.

"We're heading down to the beach. You want to join us?" Gail asked.

"No thanks. It's my birthday, and I have to stick around the house," I replied.

Gail and Julie exchanged a knowing glance, and then Gail got closer to me and whispered, "Since it's your birthday, do you want to have some fun?"

My curiosity was piqued. "What do you mean?"

Gail began to unwrap the spiral of her beach blanket. Nestled inside the roll were tiny bottles filled with different colored liquids.

"What's that?" I asked.

"We stole some liquor out of our parents' liquor cabinet. We're going for a swim and then a bike ride out in the country to drink them. It's your birthday ... you should join us," Julie said, challenging me.

"Sure, why not?" I said, feeling the exact opposite of my macho bravado.

"Try to get some liquor from your parents' stash too and we'll pick you up when we're done swimming," Julie said.

"No problem," I said, thinking this sounded better than spending my thirteenth birthday hanging around the house making frosting with my mom or playing basketball by myself with a geriatric cheering section.

I watched as Gail and Julie rode their bikes down the street a few blocks and entered the yacht club. As they rode through the entrance, the tall pines seemed to absorb them like quicksand. Too bad the sand spit them back out a short time later.

When they left my driveway, I ran to the kitchen, found some old olive and pimento jars, and quickly turned toward the liquor cabinet. My mom was down in the basement doing laundry, so I knew I had some time to sneak the booze. For some reason, I felt compelled to succeed in the mission Gail and Julie had bestowed upon me.

I opened the cupboard and there before me was a full array of bottles. I really didn't know what they were, except that my mom and dad poured quite a bit of the brown liquid into a glass when making their daily manhattans, or old fashions. Occasionally I saw the clear stuff used in making martinis.

nelly

Not knowing what to bring, I thought the smartest thing to do would be to take a little bit from each bottle. That way, no one would notice any sizable amount taken from any one bottle. Julie and Gail showed me a couple of small bottles about the size of an airplane mini-liquor bottle that they had confiscated. I wanted to show the girls that I was all in on this plan and I could outdo their stash. Like it was a competition or something.

I must have filled five or six four-to-six-ounce containers with a variety of vodka, brandy, bourbon, whiskey, and gin. There was nothing but top-shelf booze in my parents' cabinet for entertaining purposes. Whether it was self-entertainment or for others.

Little did I know what I was doing, but I felt a sense of adventure being sneaky and not getting caught. I examined the cupboard booze bottles and decided no-one would be able to tell anything was missing. They may have lost a quarter inch in volume—nothing that would be noticeable to my parents.

I took my lunch box from school and carefully aligned the bottles, cushioning them in paper towels so they wouldn't clink as I carried it away to my bike. I placed the precious cargo in my side bike basket and waited for the return of Gail and Julie by nervously shooting some hoops.

After they picked me up and we had ridden several miles, we turned off on a graveled road. It appeared that they had a particular drinking place in mind. I'm sure this wasn't their first run at this type of illicit activity.

We left our bikes and hiked a little way further into the canopied woods, thick with red and jack pines. As we got deeper into the woods, the sunny day switched to muted grayness. It was so quiet. Only the occasional scurry of a squirrel or chirp of a bird was there amidst the crunch of our shoes on the dried pine needles and fallen branches. The smell of pine permeated the senses, similar in nature to the gin I had poured a short time ago.

We stopped at four prearranged sideways tree logs, inviting us to plop down as you would around a northern campfire roasting marshmallows for s'mores. We sat and made small talk as strangers often do when they have nothing in common. It was just like being at an office Christmas party, only I was the only nervous party goer. Gail and Julie were as steady and confident as the logs we were sitting on. Shortly after we sat down, the bottles rolled out.

We decided to share what we had confiscated. Each bottle met a pair of lips and then was passed to the next person. I'll never forget the first taste of alcohol. Most girls grow up remembering when they lost their virginity. That had already been taken from me years before, so this became my "first" memorable experience.

As the rim of the jar met my lips, I took a sizable gulp, like I would normally do when drinking pop or milk. The amber liquid slid down my throat, burning my esophagus. As it entered my stomach, I almost choked. I did gag initially, which made Julie chuckle. The taste was horribly foreign. It felt like I was ingesting gasoline. Julie was watching me with the same intensity she had watched me with in the classroom, making sure I was following through with swallowing the liquid poison. I couldn't let her see my immediate dislike of the stuff. After the first few sips and exchange of bottles, I discovered that the booze went down much easier.

A slow course of alcohol went through my system, warming me from the inside out like a post-menopausal hot flash. I was immediately transformed from a bundle of nervous energy to a calm, tranquil pool. Before drinking, it was like I lived as a burn victim ... nerve endings raw and exposed to the painful world. With the alcohol in my system, it was as if those nerve endings were bathed in the sweet and soothing relief of an aloe balm.

I don't have any insight as to how I got home that day. I do remember falling off my bike a couple times without getting seriously hurt. All I had to do was keep my head up and pump my legs. Usually a bike ride was second nature to me, but on this day, I had to concentrate on riding like it was my first awkward experience. The front of my bike wobbled back and forth, and I willed myself to stay on the seat like a horseback rider would in a gallop. The next thing I knew, I was at the bottom of those garage steps, head bowed in silent prayer.

My mother never mentioned a word about me missing my birthday or sleeping twenty-four hours straight. Had she checked in on me during my slumbering hiatus, I'm sure my room would have smelled like a distillery. Yet no one really seemed to care.

My first experience with alcohol that day made me glow from the inside out. My quiet shyness transformed into gregariousness. My once serious nature became fun-loving and carefree. My Type A personality became "who the fuck cares, anyway." I liked it. A lot. That day in the woods, Glinda was born. Happy birthday to us both!

CHAPTER 8

GLINDA

If you google "Glinda," the image of Billie Burke playing Glinda the Good Witch of the North in *The Wizard of Oz* pops up immediately. Curly locks of ginger surround a smiling, pleasant face. A sparkling crown of silver adorns her cocked head. Glittered, puffy, sheer sleeves sit atop a pinkish bodice, giving her an ethereal look. A diamond-studded star wand balanced lightly in her hands finishes off the good witch's magical ensemble.

Being a "good witch" is a contradictory term. The expression "witch" connotes evil, and "good" is a positive concept. To me, Glinda has the same "ying and yang" feel to it. Everything good in my life has been because of my experience with Glinda. Everything bad has been because of her as well. Like Jeffry, Glinda lives deep within me.

The image of Glinda first came to me via a man I once worked with named Harry. Harry was an openly gay man working in a very conservative, Catholic-run hospital system. I'm not sure how Harry's gay lifestyle flew by the nuns, but somehow it was overlooked. Harry was in an administrative position at the hospital and highly successful.

Shorter in stature, brown hair clipped short, and brown wire-rimmed spectacles on a rounded face, he'd strut down the hospital corridors with purpose to his shortened stride. Often you could hear his loud cackle as he conversed with a physician, employee, or another administrator. His laughter was contagious, and if you heard it, you'd smile. Everyone who knew Harry loved him.

I'm not sure how our paths initially crossed, but I do remember going out for lunch early in our friendship. We were sitting at a cafe table with a bouquet of breadsticks before us. Our conversation, business in nature, came to a halt as the individual breadsticks slowly wilted before our eyes. We looked at each other, then back at the breadsticks, then back at each other, and then started to roar with laughter. I guess we both saw the perverted humor in a group of phallic symbols suddenly going limp.

Shortly after the luncheon, Harry had to go out of town. Upon his return, I bought breadsticks and put WELCOME BACK in doughy letters across his expansive mahogany desk for him to see as he entered his office. He must have found it comical, because soon after that we became good friends.

One Monday afternoon while I was at my desk working, I got a call from Harry. He said that he and the other administrators had decided to charter a boat and wanted to know if I'd join them for a fishing expedition on the bay of Green Bay. It was a hot, sunny, summer day, so of course I agreed. I hurried home, gathered what I needed for the charter, and left a note on the counter for my husband. The note simply said, "Gone fishing!"

The expedition was great fun. It was me and six other men my age, all hospital administrators. We were drinking beer, smoking cigars, and catching fish. It beat work any day. When I got home after midnight, my husband was not at all happy with me … or Harry, for that matter.

Years and several moves later, I got an email from Harry. It was around Thanksgiving, and he had just turned forty. His email indicated that he had been diagnosed with a brain tumor. True to his nature, Harry took on this challenge with great dignity, openness, optimism, and a sense of humor. I would get periodic email updates from him. Early on he termed his brain tumor "Glinda." He was going to beat Glinda, defeat Glinda, and destroy Glinda. Glinda had different plans, and one and a half years later, Harry died.

I know that if I passed away tomorrow, my family would mourn and be sad. I highly doubt that years after my death people would still be posting remarks on my Facebook page. They do for Harry. These are the types of sentiments people write to this day:

> *Thinking about you today again … summer reminds me of you. I think I hear your laughter in the wind.*

> *You have given me so many gifts over the years I can never repay. Your song is in my soul.*

> *Passed a garden full of sunflowers today and they made me think of you. Naturally they weren't as beautiful as your soul. You still shine amongst us!*

> *Miss you every day!. Sometimes it seems like forever since I've heard your laugh. I still tell your stories, and when I have to make a difficult decision, I try to think what would you do?*

> *Your beautiful soul is another year older, and I miss you more than ever. I bet you are running heaven by now!*

> *Not a day goes by that I don't wish you were around to share it with! I will miss you forever!*

Harry was a man who made his mark on everyone he met. He was forty-two years old when Glinda extinguished his light here in the physical world.

I have decided to carry the Glinda torch to this day. My Glinda was born that drinking day out in the woods. Truthfully, she has been with me since the day I was born, and she will be with me until I die. What I do with her in between those two points is really where the magic lies.

Although my Glinda is not a brain tumor, I was born with a significant brain disorder. The mesolimbic pathway in my brain was not formed correctly at birth. This is the area of my brain that has to do with pleasure and mood regulation. The neuroscience behind mental health issues are not always clear-cut, but instead of repeating the phrase, "my disorder associated with the mesolimbic system in my brain," I will fondly refer to my brain disorder as "Glinda" in memory of Harry and in the spirit of continuing the fight.

I compare my brain disorder to a brain tumor. The area of defect in my brain causes me to act, behave, think, and respond differently than a normal person ... much like someone with a brain tumor. Add alcohol or any other substances to the mix, and things get real dicey. Glinda causes me to do things a normal person just wouldn't do.

Early in my career as a cancer nurse, I took care of many brain tumor patients. I remember one incident with a patient as clearly as if it happened yesterday.

I'd been assigned to care for Beatrice, a retired elementary school teacher whose brain tumor had progressed in recent months. I had gotten her cares done and medications administered for the day. Right before the end of my shift as I was making last rounds to check on my patients, I passed Beatrice's door. As I looked in her room, the first thing I saw was sunlight gleaming off her bald head. I was almost past her door when I did a double take. I backed up and looked into her room. There she was sitting buck naked in her chair! She looked at me with a huge, vacant grin on her face as she continued singing nursery rhymes. I'm sure if she had been in her right mind she would have been mortified. Instead, she was sitting there very content, oblivious to her state of mind.

So for all the Harrys, Beatrice's, and those suffering from the ill effects of any sort of brain disorder, I, Nelly Anderson, continue to fight the good fight with and against the Glinda's in this world.

CHAPTER 9

CHILDREN

Similar to Beatrice, I found a passion for children early in life. It was in the Anderson blood. I cannot count the number of my family members who went into teaching children as a career. My father, sister, cousins, aunts, and grandmother all became teachers or educators in their professional careers, trying to be positive influences on the next generation.

After that summer in the woods, my teen years involved summer jobs around disadvantaged children. My father would get me jobs filling in as an assistant for summer kids' programs at school. One summer I assisted special needs children. These were kids with developmental delays, Down syndrome, or behavioral problems.

I will never forget one little girl, aged six, named Jennifer. At first, Jennifer was very cautious around me, but by the end of the first week, she stuck to me like glue. She wore wire-rimmed glasses surrounding eyes the color of the sky. She had bangs and dish-water blonde hair that she wore pulled back in a high ponytail. Her teeth were crooked and yellowing, but her smile lit up the room. Her giggle was infectious. She was happy and joyous all the time. Her soul shined.

nelly

I developed a fierce need to protect these kids. They were vulnerable yet inspiring to me. Despite their limitations, they never gave up on developing even the smallest of skills. Despite their individual handicaps, they took pride and were happy with any small step forward they made. I learned as much from them as they learned from me ... perhaps more.

Because of my exposure to these "less than perfect" humans, I developed a deep sense that abortion was wrong. How could anyone abort a child when one of them might turn out to be a pure blessing?

During English class one day, we were given a writing assignment that was to reflect our belief system or personal values on a certain subject. I chose the topic of abortion and wrote the following poem from the embryo's perspective.

Without a Chance

From the confines of my room,
I view the outside world in bloom
And feel the happiness sublime
Surrounding me and all that's mine.

For not too long ago was I
Anything more than a mere lie,
A nonexistent entity,
A mistake that never should be.

There was a time you loved so well,
A blissful instance not to tell;
At that time you made for me
A beginning, end, and between.

But as for now I shall lay still,
A prisoner in my chamber cell,
Protected by a guard so fair,
Who made me from a love affair.

Until the time when I escape,
The binds that hold me then will break,
And release to this kind world
A born child ... unloved, unprocured.

Why must we have to suffer so?
We little ones shan't ever know
A zest for life, for it is spurn
Away from us ne'er to return.

But what is life: if you'll not be
Happy and free, disjoined from me.
I can't be your responsibility!

I received a good grade on the poem. Feeling a sense of pride, I shared it with my mother. A torrent of tears ensued. There was one night in my life that my father took care of us kids. My mother was having minor female surgery. She'd had an abortion. After I found out, I didn't talk to her for months.

CHAPTER 10

STEVE

Staring at a photograph from 1976 brings a smile to my face. The picture was taken in the living room at our house close to the beach and yacht club. There is gold carpeting throughout the living room. A couch my Grandma Helga is sitting on is light and dark gold striped with large matching striped cushions marking the perimeter.

My grandmother, always in a dress, has on a light aqua button-up fitted frock with a string of pearls at her neck. Behind her is a large, sand-colored brick fireplace with a wooden mantle. Visible in the photo is the flickering of golden flames against the bowels of the black fire pit. A picturesque, cozy winter day ... close to Christmas, as I recall.

My elegant grandmother is in the background of the photo, sitting on the couch and holding a gallon jug of port wine. She is wearing an impish grin on her face as she stares at the camera lens. She looks like a little kid that got caught with her hand in the cookie jar as she hangs on to her bottle like it's a lifeline.

In the forefront of the picture is my high school boyfriend, Steve, wearing jeans and a blue and white striped shirt. He is lying on his belly with his elbows on the ground propping up his upper body. Next to him is my mother, her right arm around Steve's neck. She is lying on her left side. Not only are they locked in an embrace, but their eyes are closed and they are locking lips as well. No doubt I am the one taking the picture, and I'm sure it was staged and meant to be humorous at the time. To me, however, it symbolically represents the level of dysfunction in the family.

My first relationship with the opposite sex was with Steve. He became my best friend in the eighth grade. We dated for four years. My sister, Susie, also dated a boy named Steve throughout high school. It made for interesting phone calls, not knowing which Steve wanted which Anderson girl.

Steve and I grew up together from the ages of fourteen to seventeen. He was a year older than me. He was very personable, and everyone liked him ... including my mother, as you may have guessed! Steve was known as a jock, and I was the Brainiac.

Since that day in the woods, Glinda had remained at bay. I stayed on the straight and narrow, concentrating on school and getting good grades. I became president of the school National Honor Society, first chair clarinet player, and class officer. I received medals at state, took college preparatory classes, and was on the swim team. My sister and I both graduated valedictorian of our respective classes. We received multiple educational scholarships. Perfection expected and professionally executed by the Anderson girls.

The other part of my life revolved around Steve. He was a star basketball, football, and tennis player. I watched him play sports and was there for him after big wins to help celebrate at Brother's Three Pizza or Mickey Lou's hamburger joint. His friends became my friends and we double-dated a lot with his jock friends and their cheerleader girlfriends.

The relationship had the usual teenage sexual experimentation, spats, and jealous moments, but mainly we were best friends. Later in life, he told me he had saved all my letters, graduation picture, and a few mementos. Amongst the stack was his favorite—a red, heart-shaped valentine that I had written for him. Within the red heart construction paper was another white heart outlined with a red felt pen. On the inside with red lettering was written:

You are the only guy for me. I hope that this
is plain to see. That all these years I've loved you much,
and still am longing for each touch. As time goes on there
forms a bond, so special that no-one dare break it.
And I want you to know that even though,
through miles we are now
apart. You're so
close to me
within my
HEART!

CHAPTER 11

DESTRUCTION

Somewhere around the age of sixteen the bottom started falling out of my life. My mother decided it was time to get a job now that her kids were growing up, so she became a realtor and started working. The house felt empty and cold without her in it when I came home from school.

That same year, my sister left for college. In my senior year, Steve left for California. The night Steve left, I cried all night long. I felt as if a part of me had died. Often during this time my father would come out of board meetings to find that his tires had been slashed. He'd also get phone calls threatening his life. I guess education had become a dangerous business, even back in the late 1970s. It was a tense time both inside our home and in the community.

At 6:00 a.m. one day, the shrill of the alarm awakened me out of the last of my hazy dreams. Shaking off the remnants of sleep, I plodded out to the kitchen where my mom had set the table festively for morning breakfast with green braided placemats set with yellow and brown rimmed crockery. Plates with three bright daisies floating in the middle were meant to be a cheery way to start the day.

nelly

My father looked at me through bleary, red eyes from the opposite end of the table, dropping Alka Seltzer into his glass to start the day. As the *plop-plop fizz-fizz* escalated, he began his usual mantra about how perfect he was and how he hoped I would continue on the same path. Reassuring him, I seemed to settle his angst as the Alka Seltzer settled his belly. At the same time, my mom stood at her post at the stove, throwing daggers my father's way. The revulsion she emoted toward him was palpable.

As the bread sprang from the toaster and was placed atop the daisies, my stomach growled and became nauseous all at once. I stuffed the warm, coarse bread into my mouth. As my mother busied herself with her morning routine, my father went on about his perfection, sipping his morning antacid cocktail. I spit the toast into my napkin and threw it away as I cleared my dishes.

As I began my school day in homeroom, I'd often chat with Mr. L., our homeroom teacher and art instructor. He also happened to be a family friend. That day he greeted me as usual.

"How are you doing today, Nelly?"

"Okay. What are you working on?" I asked as orange paint met canvas.

"I'm making a painting for you," he replied.

"Wow, thanks," I said.

"Say, sorry to hear your dad got picked up last night," Mr. L. continued.

"What do you mean?" I asked.

"I heard your dad got a DUI last night. Your poor mom is such a nice lady, she doesn't deserve what she's getting."

"Yeah, I guess," I said and scampered off to my seat, feeling the same grinding nausea in the pit of my stomach. I wasn't sure what I was supposed to do with such a statement.

Taking college preparatory classes required me to spend half my lunch hour in the library studying. After a half hour of cramming, I'd head to the large commons, which was an open area with various sized tables for lunch. It accommodated the entire student body at the same time, so it was noisy and frenetic.

The lunch line was on one side, and glassed-in administrative offices lined the other. The gym was off to one side behind a wall of heavy wooden doors. Brightly painted orange, red, yellow, and green lockers and ramps leading to two levels of classrooms rounded out the fourth side of the commons area.

My lunch consisted of a piece of cinnamon sugar-free gum. I would sit with friends and say I had already eaten and just socialize the rest of the time before afternoon classes resumed.

Often as we sat in the commons, we would hear a low rumble of voices begin to stir. We would immediately know what was coming. A woman who worked in the guidance office would come strutting across the dining hall. She was probably five to ten years older than my parents. She wore clingy, knit, low-cut dresses that hung many inches above her knee. She had large breasts and skinny, bird-like legs.

The low rumble of voices would become audible as this secretary sashayed across the high school commons after getting her lunch. As she headed back to her office, the kids would hit their hands on the lunch tables and chant, "Boom-boom, boom-boom," in rhythm with her strutting steps and bouncing breasts. I don't know what her actual name was. Everyone referred to her as "Boom-boom."

On that day I decided to get up and follow her into the guidance office. Even though I never participated in the jeering, I felt discomfited for the woman. I also felt disgusted at the entire student body.

"I'm so sorry you have to be around these idiots," I said to the secretary as she shimmied her buttocks in the back of her desk chair.

"It's okay, I just ignore them," she said in a small, breathy voice. "Are you here to see Dave?" she asked me quietly.

"Yes, I'm still not sure if I want to go into teaching, special ed., or nursing, and I thought I could review my latest aptitude tests to see if he could help steer me in one direction or another," I stated.

"Well, you will be successful, no matter what you choose to do. I know it," she said with a flat grin. "Dave is busy this aft, so you might want to try another day."

Truth be told, I really felt sorry for this woman. I tried to treat her with dignity and respect. As I left the office, I gave her a big smile and wave. Her thin lips ended up in a straight line—the best she could do for a smile, I guess. With downcast eyes, she gave a short wave back. As I walked into the commons, I could feel her eyes following me as I got swept up in the stream of kids heading toward the ramps to their afternoon classes.

After school, I was sitting at our dinner table doing homework as my mother sauntered through the door. Dressed in rust-colored trousers and her gold Century 21 blazer, she looked like a giant walking hot dog dripping in mustard. Her face and extremities were the color of a white, pasty bun. I took one look at her and knew something was terribly wrong.

"What happened?" I said.

"Nothing," she replied as she sprinted for the half bathroom off the kitchen. She started to run water in the sink. I could hear the vomiting spasms over the blast of the spigot. Several minutes passed and then I heard muffled short sobs begin.

"Mom, what happened?" I asked more forcefully, knocking on the bathroom door.

She opened the door, hobbled to the kitchen table, and sat down heavily. Tears were brimming and threatening to spill onto the table.

"I just got a box delivered to my office," she said.

"Well, what was in it?"

"Items of your dad's clothes, like his underwear and T-shirts. Cards and love notes he had written to another woman," she replied.

The gnawing pain and nausea hit me again "From who?" I asked.

"Some secretary at the high school."

"Oh my God, not ... Boom-boom!" I blurted out.

But in the twist of fate that was my life, it was Boom-boom. My perfect father had engaged in a five-year affair with the school floozy. Everyone in town knew it but us.

That night in bed I was awakened by my mom's hushed voice and my dad's loud voice.

"I don't care if I wake up Nelly," my dad said. "Bring her out here to settle this if you want."

My mom's hushed tones and pleading voice tried to get his drunken behavior under control. Trying to reason with a drunk is like trying to talk to a deaf person. It just doesn't work on any level. As they fought at the kitchen table, I lay in bed on the other side of the wall, doing a thousand sit-ups as tears streamed down my face.

Working on the marriage … then not … became a two-year focus for my parents. My dad's drinking escalated, and so did my mom's. I was used as the intermediary between the two of them. Sometimes I was sent by my mom to spy on my dad to see if he was still seeing Boom-boom. I would sit parked for hours on a rural road trying to espy his blue and white Oldsmobile coming or going from Boom-boom's house, and then report back to Georgia my findings. Then I would be asked by my dad to try to smooth things over with my mom for him. I felt like a shuttlecock, the missile-like feather contraption used in badminton, bouncing from one side of the marriage to the other.

The bottom was falling out from under me, the earth's foundation cracking quickly below my feet. Chaos and uncertainty had become my life. Everything that I knew as security was fast dissolving.

One day I was looking through a magazine and saw how skinny the beautiful models were in the pictures. I decided I wanted to be like them and look "perfect" as well. Maybe if I could achieve perfection, my parents wouldn't fight. Maybe they had problems because I wasn't perfect enough like my dad.

That day I ordered some advertised diet pills from the same magazine sporting flawless women. I started to take diet pills on top of continuing to eat minimally, and the weight began falling off. I obsessed over every morsel I put into my mouth, and I weighed myself religiously. As I watched the dial of the scale go lower and lower, I got "high" on the feeling of grasping an unattainable standard. Glinda was hard at work.

I began drinking diet pop for breakfast to fill up my empty belly. That along with the piece of gum for lunch would tide me over until I got home from school. After school, I was self-allotted a certain amount of sweets, like Twinkies or sandwich cookies. I became ritualistic in how I consumed food.

When eating a Twinkie, I'd scrape off the outer layer of dark, spongy goodness with my two front teeth first. Next, I'd cut it exactly in half and lick out the white creamy center with one swoop of the tongue. First one half, then the other. Finally, I could begin on the rest of the Twinkie. I had to nibble all around the outside of the two halves, not breaking into the center where the filling had been. After squirreling away the outside, the final *piece de resistance* was the spongy middle mixed in with whatever creamy goodness remained. If I didn't get the ritual done correctly, I'd give myself a mental lashing.

I would be sneaky. If I had to eat with my mother, I'd cut up whatever was for dinner into a hundred small bites so that it looked like I was eating more than I was. I'd push around on the plate more than I put into my mouth. The more she encouraged me to eat, the less I did. It was the only control I had over my disintegrating life.

My mother would have meals in the crock pot for when I got home from school, and I would take plates of it and grind it up in the garbage disposal, telling her how delicious it was when she got home from work. I delved into school work and all my activities with renewed fervor.

While I was running on fumes, Glinda was swallowing them and gaining steam. I would look at my body in the mirror and see a fat person, even when skeletal bones began protruding. I started out at five-feet-six and weighed a hundred and thirty pounds, which was probably on the slender side. It wasn't good enough for me. I wanted to be thinner, so I continued to starve myself and self-destruct. The thinner I got, the more I approached nirvana in my mind's eye.

My dad was kicked out of the house for good one month before I graduated from high school. Upon my valedictorian triumphant graduation, I weighed ninety-five pounds. I had dark circles around my eyes, sunken cheeks, and visible cartilage bands of my trachea beneath my chin. I looked like a Holocaust victim.

My mother, obviously concerned about my appearance, took me to a shrink … against my will. The following is an excerpt from that evaluation:

> Nelly gave a history of progressive weight loss to the point of amenorrhea and is beginning to endanger herself with her illness. This illness is certainly related to the impending divorce and the family stress that has gone on the last two years.
>
> I was impressed with Nelly being fairly emotionally stable and a reasonable girl, and I have a feeling she will pull out of this condition. However, a certain percentage of young girls do develop an illness called anorexia nervosa, in which there is severe weight loss to the point of damage to their bodies and endocrine disturbance. It is too early to tell if Nelly is going to fall into this group, and there is no way to predict that at this point. However, we would say there is a possibility that this severe illness could occur and she would need longer term psychiatric and medical care.

This psych visit report was carbon copied to my mom's lawyers. She was using my mental state and anorexic condition to prove to the court the trauma caused by my father's philandering behavior, allowing her to recoup maximum financial gain from the divorce settlement. So much for the health and well-being of your kid.

In 1977, my parents decided to divorce. Dad decided to marry Boom-boom. My mom was distraught, scared about her future, and drinking alcohol excessively. Susie was off at college and oblivious to the family struggles. Steve was attending college in California, and we missed each other terribly. I was self-destructing at an alarming pace.

Glinda was doing her job. She was the only happy one, and she was just getting started!

CHAPTER 12

FRIDAY

One Friday morning in homeroom, Mr. L. handed me an eight by ten canvassed piece of artwork mounted on wood for hanging purposes. On it was a caricature of me he had painted.

My face had an exaggerated piano-keyed grin and pronounced bony facial features. My body was portrayed as a tapered, orange carrot. The writing underneath stated: "If I only eat vegetables, I will start looking like one!" Along with having bizarre eating habits and rituals, I had begun my vegetarian phase.

With Steve out in California during my senior year, I needed to fill that void in my life, so I developed some close female friends. That was another first for me … and what a fun discovery! There were three of us that hung around together on Friday nights.

Every week, Sara's little black Mustang would roar into my driveway. Kathy would already be in the passenger seat of the car. I'd move Kathy's bucket seat forward and climb into the back, settling into my spot in the middle between the two front seats. I'd perch my bony butt on the edge of the seat and assume my riding position so that I could easily chat with both friends as well as look through the front windshield to observe where we were going. Like a small child, I didn't want to miss anything along the joyride. Doing "the loop" around our city and the adjacent city became a Friday night ritual.

As if by magic, the car would take us to our first stop, which was our "stash" of liquor. Having an eighteen-year-old friend in 1977 came in handy, because she could legally buy booze. The three of us would get paid our meager wages from after-school jobs, and Sara promptly went out to buy a large volume of alcohol.

Our liquor repository became a favorite grassy field on the edge of town. There we would retrieve the fermented liquid each Friday night. A well-worn foot path would lead from the road straight to the stockpile, but by Saturday morning, Mother Nature had restored the trampled ground to its original grassy knoll. No one was the wiser. If a wino had accidentally stumbled across our reserves, he would have thought he'd won the lottery!

After retrieving our spirits and getting back into the car, Sara would hand me my bottle of T.J. Swan's Easy Nights. Sara and Kathy preferred the taste of Mellow Days, so each of us ended up with our own cheap, green wine bottle and Styrofoam cup. Sitting on my perch, I couldn't get my bottle top unscrewed fast enough.

My raw nervous energy would diminish after the wine started to flow, and I'd soon feel the soothing blanket of alcohol I'd discovered years ago that summer in the woods. With each swallow, tranquility set in.

After driving around "the loop" chatting, laughing, and drinking, we'd go to parties, dances, the local roller rink, or sneak into an outdoor movie theater. Whatever happened to be "happening" in a small Midwestern town on a Friday night—which usually wasn't much—we would be there!

I would transform from a seriously proper person by day to an outgoing, fun-loving, do-anything-I-want kind of girl by night. Although I didn't have a split personality like Dr. Jekyll and Mr. Hyde, my behavior and moral compass drastically changed when drinking alcohol.

After a drinking episode, we'd think nothing of playing dine and dash. We considered raiding and destroying someone's produce gardens or property as kids just being kids. We were never caught doing anything abhorrent. Again, behavior with no consequences. As T.J. Swan promised, by ingesting the wine, my nights became so much easier.

CHAPTER 13

COLLEGE

Returning to the town of my birth, my mom and I pulled up to the four story, brown brick, L-shaped building called Sutherland Hall at the University of Wisconsin-Eau Claire (UWEC). This would be my new school-year home.

I scanned the outdoor landscape. There were college kids milling about, and some were playing tennis or volleyball on the nearby courtyards. Kids were throwing Frisbees in the open expanse of upper campus fields.

"I can't wait to meet my roommate," I said to my mother. At least as incoming freshman we could figure out this new chapter in life together. Whether we even would like each other I didn't much care. I just wanted to have someone in the same boat as me, feeling as vulnerable and afraid to take this next giant life step.

"I'm sure she will be nice," my mother replied robotically.

We came to a stop, and my dampened hand quickly pushed open the car door. I looked over at my mother and saw silent tears streaming down her face. My eyes, unusually dry for such an occasion, looked to the ground as I said quietly, "You can just drop me off; no need to come in."

"Are you sure you'll be okay?" my mother asked.

I launched my ninety-five pounds out the car door like a bullet and said with unfelt bravado, "Of course, I'll be fine!"

Like slamming a book closed after a good read, the car door shut with a pneumatic *thump*. I felt a sense of satisfaction being done with that chapter of my life. It was as if a weight lifted from my shoulders, and I thought to myself, *At least one of us will be fine.*

I also felt a sense of guilt leaving Georgia alone. I had become her caretaker throughout the divorce. She clung to me like a lifeline. It was like both of us were being forced to take giant new steps in our lives and needed to be apart to chart our own courses.

Unlike high school classmates of mine who buddied up with friends and went off to the same college, I knew no one going to UWEC. Unless you counted my sister. She was a junior and living off campus in one of the student rentals. She was off getting settled in her own house with her long-ago established college friends.

Feeling like a fish out of water, I traversed the pale blue hallways of Sutherland Hall with a box of room decor in tow. I navigated up the steps to find my new home on 2 north. As I came close to my assigned room, the butterflies in my stomach began to flutter. I would finally meet my new roommate!

As I neared the room, I heard high-pitched female voices and laughter—clearly friends reuniting from a long summer apart. There were hugs and loud chatter in the hallway, and "Margaritaville" was blaring loudly on someone's stereo. You could smell the fresh fall air mingled with the musty smell of old books. The excitement and electricity amongst the girls was palpable.

Taking a deep breath and closing my eyes, I timidly knocked on the door of my assigned room. The door opened halfway, and I sidled into the room, which was about the size of my bedroom back home.

Shelly, my new roommate, was there to greet me. Outgoing, athletic, beautiful, bouncy, nasal-voiced Shelly. After brief introductions,

I thought I had really lucked out. She seemed great and gave off the aura of being completely comfortable in these new surroundings.

We weren't alone in the room, however. Shelly was surrounded by a small group of friends. It turned out she was a sophomore. The whole block of 2 north girls were sophomores. So much for being in the same boat with another newbie. I felt totally alone.

After introductions, Shelly and her posse decided to go out and find additional friends from freshman year, so I was left alone to get settled in my new home. I started the familiar task of making up my bed and decorating my side of the room. Putting up a few posters and making up the flimsy cot that was my bed took little time. There was a closet the size of a broom closet where I hung up my entire year's wardrobe. I put cosmetics and toiletries in the wooden upholstered shelving above my bed and plopped my newly acquired textbooks on my desk. Moving in accomplished in record time!

Although the two sides of the room were mirror images of each other, Shelly's side looked polished, and mine looked cobbled. It all felt a bit eclectic and not too homey, but it would have to do for now.

After a half hour I was officially settled. *Now what am I supposed to do?* I decided to go wandering around the second floor to get a feel for the place. I passed through the part of the building labeled "center" and began winding around the L-shaped building to 2 west. Each block was just that—a square block of rooms with a community bathroom and shower combination in the middle of the block.

I sauntered around the blocks, snooping in open dorm rooms as I passed. Some kids had families helping them unpack and decorate. Some girls had boyfriends helping them haul larger items into their rooms. Many had friends assisting them and would gather in tearful hugs to say goodbye.

As I made my way around the last corner of 2 west on my way back to my room, I saw a girl sitting in the hallway, her back against a closed dorm room door. Her head was bent between her knees. Cascading brown, curly locks flowed over pitched legs. Shoulders were heaving and sound of muffled sobs emitted from the tops of her kneecaps.

I immediately ran up to her, tapped her right shoulder and asked if she was okay.

She slowly looked up at me with wet, brown eyes, caked make-up running down her face in the tracks of her tears, and blubbered, "No. I don't want to be here. I don't know a single person."

"I know what you mean," I responded empathetically. "I'm Nelly, by the way, and I don't know anyone either. I live on 2 north. I'm just killing time walking around."

Her body started to uncurl from her protective ball. Wiping her tear-streaked face, she stood up and said, "Hi, I'm Tracy," as a tentative and cautious smile unfurled.

"Have you gotten your room together yet?" I asked.

"No. I don't know where to even start, and my family had to get back home."

"Well, let me help you," I offered. "I just finished my room, so I have time."

"Thanks a lot!" Tracy's tentative smile broke into a broad, beaming band of white enamel.

That was the start of a close friendship. We became inseparable during freshman year.

Tracy was exotic looking with long, brown, wavy hair; an olive complexion; big, beautiful, brown eyes; and straight, white teeth. The only thing slightly off on this beautiful creature was an abnormally shaped and sized nose; however, because she was so striking otherwise, a person tended not to notice the imperfection.

She came to UWEC from a town with a population of 300 in the middle of upper Wisconsin. Her parents were recently divorced, and her dad was a military man who wasn't really a part of her life. Our similar backgrounds cemented our friendship even further. We quickly settled into our first year of college; I was accepted into the competitive School of Nursing, and Tracy decided to study communicative disorders to become an audiologist.

Since I had taken all college preparatory courses as a senior in high school, freshman year academically was a repeat of material I had already learned, so the year became party year for Tracy and me. We went out drinking every Wednesday through Saturday nights.

Water Street was known for having the highest concentration of bars per block, so it was a place we would visit on nights out. The bars included Old Home, Stables, The Joynt, Shenanigans, and Cameraderie, to name just a few. Although one bar featured country music, another aimed more toward hard metal, another one disco, and another one was a townie bar. It was wall to wall kids.

They were all the same, smelling of sweat, old popcorn, and stale beer. Music would blare, people would talk loudly. As we made our way to the bar to get a pitcher of beer, we would usually end up being jostled and having someone spill quarter taps on our clothes or hair along the way. Waking up the next morning hungover felt horrible, and smelling like a brewery didn't help matters.

Our nightly routine would end at Shenanigans. After a night of drinking, it would be time to get out on the disco dance floor to Abba's "Dancing Queen" or the Bee Gee's "Night Fever" or "Staying Alive." Then we would head across the street to Suburpia for a tuna sub before hitting the road to hitchhike back up the hill to the dorms. If we didn't get a ride hitchhiking, we would have to climb 120 vertical steps from lower to upper campus. After a full night of drinking, dancing and carousing, we were usually too lazy for such a prospect.

One night hitchhiking, we got a ride from a blond guy in an old beat up pickup truck. He looked to be middle-aged and kind of rough around the edges. He appeared to be a craft worker with all sorts of odds and ends of parts, tools, and wood scraps in the bed of his truck. As we had done a hundred times before when hitchhiking, I got in first and sat next to the weathered man. Tracy sat by the door. The three of us crammed into the front seat of his pickup.

We started chatting, and I'm sure the guy could tell by smell alone that he had picked up two inebriated college girls. We told him we wanted to go to upper campus to our dorm. He started out being friendly, talking to us about school and what we were majoring in. A few minutes into the ride, my "Spidey sense" kicked in. Tracy silently nudged my thigh. Instead of turning right at the top of the hill heading to upper campus, this guy turned left and was heading out of town!

I sobered up immediately, and my body went into flight or fight mode. Frightened as well as somewhat irked, I confronted him.

"Where are we going?" I demanded. "We were supposed to turn right back there."

The guy didn't utter a word, but instead kept his eyes forward, staring like laser beams at the road in front of us. The truck accelerated. Tracy and I grasped hands.

We were at the edge of town. There was a gas station lit up on the right side of the road. It was like finding an oasis in the middle of the desert. A big stop sign outlined in blinking lights materialized before us at a four way stop. I could tell this guy was not going to heed the stop sign, but he did slow down significantly, turning his head from right to left to scan the intersection.

I squeezed Tracy's clammy hand. As we approached the stop sign, my eyes caught hers. Her eyes followed mine down to the door handle. In silent agreement, we were going to make a run for it.

As the guy scanned to the left, I yelled, "Jump!"

Tracy seized the door handle and shouldered the door as we both half piled out and jumped out of the cab of the truck. We ended up on the ground with me on top of Tracy. As I scurried to my feet, I turned to tug on her arm and simultaneously yelled, "Run!" The guy was fumbling with his seat belt, trying to get out of his truck and come after us. We never looked back. We sprinted our asses off to the bright lights of the welcoming gas station.

We bolted through the glass doors and startled the night cashier.

Nelly

"We were just kidnapped by a guy in a truck!" I screamed. I pointed back to an empty spot on the road bearing white exhaust silhouetted against the black of night. All three of us surveyed the road, only to see fading red taillights crawl off into the night like a vexed animal without its prey, white exhaust puffing angrily in its wake.

CHAPTER 14

DAN

One weekend after December break during our freshman year, Tracy went home to visit her family. I was asked if I wanted to tag along with my roommate, Shelly, and her friends to a frat party. I felt like the little sister they were obligated to take and babysit. I decided to go anyway.

After paying a couple of bucks to get into the party, having our hands stamped with the fraternity's emblem and given our token plastic beer cup, Shelly and her buddies trotted off to find their group of guy friends and announce their arrival. I meandered around the house until I found the throng of people surrounding the prized keg of beer. When it was my turn, I expertly depressed the lever on the end of the snake-like tubing, tilted the cup, and filled it with Bud Light. Of course, I filled the cup with as little of the white frothy head as possible, leaving an optimal amount of beer for me to drink.

Figuring the girls would return eventually, I settled into a corner and leaned against a wall to watch the party-goers. I scanned the room to see if I recognized anyone I knew from campus. I was enjoying my beer and the view when a couple older guys came up to me. One of the guys was long and lean with dark blond hair, a little on the shaggy side.

His face was long and lean as well, and his smile produced a youthful grin with dimples on each side.

The other guy was dark blond with longer, feathered-back hair, wisps of it sticking out all over like a guy that continually ran his hands through his hair out of nervous habit. He was shorter than the first guy. I found both of them very handsome and certainly friendly as they came up to me, smiling.

"Hi, do you come here often?" the shorter guy questioned.

A short giggle. "Nope, first time for me," I replied. "I'm with my roommate and her friends, but they went off to find some people to let them know we're here."

"Well, we'll keep you company if you want until they get back," the taller one said, taking a sip of his beer but keeping his eyes intently focused on mine.

"I'd like that! I'm Nelly, by the way."

"Nice to meet you," tall guy said, shaking my hand. "I'm Dan, and this little guy here is Brian."

"Nice to meet you, Dan and little guy Brian," I responded with a twinkle in my eye and a flirtatious shake of Brian's hand.

We chatted for some time, batting the routine questions back and forth. Where are you from? What year? What classes? What professors? Where living? Dan seemed very down to earth and friendly. He was an easy conversationalist and made you feel like you had known him forever. He hung on every word I said and maintained eye contact as if we were the only two people in the room.

Brian was a bundle of sheer energy. He was equivalent in personality to a Jack Russell terrier—high strung, pent up energy, about to explode. As suspected, he did rake his hands through his hair constantly. Brian was an amusing conversationalist. As we chitchatted, a steady stream of partygoers passed by, waving or saying hi to Brian. It seemed like everyone at the party knew him. Later that night, I discovered why. Brian had his own radio talk show on campus called "Kato and Friends". Later in life, he was known as O.J. Simpson's famous "Houseguest", Kato Kaelin!

The one-liners Brian threw out in normal conversation had you belly laughing. As you were recovering from one zinger, he'd let the next one fly even funnier than the one before. By the time Dan, Brian, and I had finished our first beer and were recovering from Brian's entertainment, Shelly and company were snaking their way toward us.

"Hey, Dan; hey, Brian," Shelly said with her nasal twang. "How are you guys?"

"You know these guys?" I quizzed Shelly as I fisted my hand and pointed my thumb toward Dan and Brian.

"Sure, we all went to Nicolet together, so I've known them since high school," Shelly chimed in.

Dan and I began dating and fell in love. Hard and fast. He was from an upscale suburb of Milwaukee called Bayside. Until this point, Steve and I had maintained a semi-long distant relationship, seeing each other whenever we could, which wasn't often. I called him in California and said I had met someone else. We called it quits for good, and I began dating Dan the next day.

Dan made everything magically okay for me. I was happy again. I began to eat, although I was still a vegetarian. I put some meat on my bones. It felt as if my world that had been tilted for so long was suddenly righted and spinning on course again. We dated for two years and had a wonderful time.

Summers were really hard to be away from each other with Dan in Milwaukee and me in Eau Claire at nursing school. We tried to see each other whenever possible. All we could do back in the late '70s was write each other letters and talk on the phone. I would receive one to two letters a week when we were apart. Some of the excerpts from the letters he sent to me were:

Nelly

Nelly,

Thank you very, very much for a fantastic weekend! It was just great. It really is much better if I can get up there to see you; we get a lot more time to ourselves. I'll say one thing. I got a lot more time staying in bed this weekend than any other, but I got a lot less sleep, and I won't complain about that ... remember, you are my life, and I love you with all my heart. Keep the faith. All my love. Dan

I am possibly in the lowest and most depressed mood of the whole summer. I'll run down my list quickly. I hate work; I'm sick of school; I'm mad at the mailman for not bringing your letter, thus keeping me in suspense; I'm bored out of my mind; and I love you more than anything in the world and I can't be with you! I just wanted to get a letter this weekend to you to let you know that you are the most important thing happening in my life, and I'm not ever going to let you go!! Take heed of my warning. I love you with all my heart and then some!

Dan

Nelly,

Well, today is your birthday, and I am very sorry I can't be there to celebrate it with you ... hopefully it won't be long before we see each other again—my heart is set on a week and two days. I am taking things in stride now and handling things much better. I'm even working out again. I still need one person to tie everything together for me—YOU!! I'm thinking about you all the time. I love you.

Always,

Dan

Tonight I had a talk with my parents about graduate school. I am pumped now ... Nelly, the one thing that does bum me out is to hear you talk about marriage the way you do. I don't know what to think. I realize you have gone through a very traumatic experience, which I could never even come close to understanding, so I know you have reasons for feeling the way you do ... you cannot lose your faith in marriage.

Marriage and children are the most sacred things there are... at the time you've found the person that you love enough to marry, you'll know it. You have complete confidence that that person is who you'd like to spend the rest of your life with, and there is no doubt that it will work out.

I know it, I've found the person I'd like to marry ... obviously, it is you! I have no doubts. When I talk to you, I can tell you are not completely sold, and that is understandable. My love for you is very solid, and I believe in you. Keep thinking of me! Yours always,

Dan

P.S. Also wanted to mention I feel you should really try wearing a pair of pants under that skimpy skirt at work. Nelly, I don't think I'll ever stop worrying about you!

Dan was a good man. He cared deeply for me and treated me well. He loved me unconditionally. He was always a gentleman. He was boyishly handsome and on course for success in life. Dan was everything a girl could and should want.

nelly

Only I wasn't a typical girl. When it got too serious, I ran scared. I wasn't used to my world being in such balance. Although for a two-year period the normality of the relationship felt good, I easily became jaded. Glinda persuaded me to say goodbye to a great man and trudge onward.

CHAPTER 15

ROOMMATES

Before junior year, seven Sutherland girls, including me, decided to hunt for off-campus housing. We found a two-story grey house at 522 Niagara Street, a mile from campus.

The house was in good shape for off-campus housing. Climbing five steps to a red front door, you would enter a small foyer that doubled as closet space for coats and shoes. From the foyer, you would step into a roomy living room with gold carpet and light entering from the front bay window. Although worn in appearance by sagging, outdated furniture, the room was bright and cheery with natural sunlight.

One small bedroom was off the living room to the left as you entered the house. Bunk beds were in that room. Past the living room and to the right was a full bathroom. To the left was a galley kitchen with bright red, white, and black striped wallpaper. Beyond the kitchen was the back bedroom with dark wood paneling and also housing bunk beds. This bedroom was dark, cold, and uninviting. There was a spacious common area in between the kitchen and living room where a large chrome-legged and Formica-topped kitchen table sat.

To the left of the common area were carpeted steps leading up to two upstairs bedrooms. There was a small single bedroom to the right at the top of the stairs, and to the left was the fourth spacious bedroom, again with bunk beds.

Other than the front door and the kitchen decor, the colors were neutral. Eggshell flat off- white paint covered the walls throughout the house, and dark brown furniture added the only drab contrast.

Tracy and I were charged with finding housing at the end of sophomore year when we stumbled upon our Niagara find. We thought it would be a perfect house for us.

"This house is great," I said. "Four bedrooms for seven of us, and plenty of living space. It would be a great party house too!"

Tracy chimed in agreement but was reluctant; pointing out that it only had one bathroom for seven people.

"Yeah, but we'll all have staggering school schedules, so we'd need it at different times anyway," I responded.

"Okay, I guess the price is right," she grudgingly agreed.

The summer between sophomore and junior year we moved into the house. The seven of us drew straws for rooms, and, luckily, I drew the straw for the single upstairs bedroom. Tracy drew the straw to share the next-door bedroom upstairs with another of our roommates.

I was the only nursing student in the house and had the most rigorous course work, so having a private room for myself turned out to be essential. The rest of my roommates were in a variety of majors, mostly education.

We hosted frequent house parties during junior year, and our house became well known as a party house, as well as a house where seven good looking girls lived. On campus, we were known as the 522 girls. There was constant activity in the house, and friends as well as guys coming and going all hours of the day and night.

Glinda continued to take precedence in my life. Although I still was able to balance school and do well academically with my partying ways, a few other Glinda behaviors surfaced. My weight started increasing due to partying and college life eating habits. My anxiety over additional pounds increased, and the tough school schedule led me down another interesting path.

My increasing anxiety caused me to overeat. I could pack away a large amount of pizza and ice cream on any given night. Then feeling extremely guilty for eating the massive amounts, I sought out the sanctuary of the bathroom. I would lean over the toilet, stick my finger down my throat, and throw up as much of the undigested food as I could.

I would immediately get a feeling of relief … another high of sorts. Purging food from my system was like purging the poison from the depths of my soul. I hated myself for eating, for puking, for just being me. Throwing in laxatives on top of purging seemed to work well to cleanse my system. I wanted my body to feel as empty as my soul. The cycle of overeating, purging, and eating again became a daily ritual. Between bulimia and excessive drinking, Glinda was very happy.

Another facet of my diseased brain caused me to look for love wherever I could find it. After a night of drinking, I would sleep around, wanting to be loved by someone … anyone. Since I didn't love myself, maybe I could make someone else love me, and thus feel whole.

Our house of Niagara girls had counterpart houses of guys with whom we would alternate partying on any given weekend. Whatever house of guys we partied with, I knew I would end up sleeping with one certain person from the group.

One group of guys lived down the road from our Niagara house and was known as the "Madison boys," from Madison, Wisconsin. Our house would meet up with their house and go out bar hopping on weekends. If we were all going out together, I knew that my night would end sleeping with Terry.

Terry, who was intelligent, loved Bob Dylan, and was a progressive-thinking man. His thoughts mainly went "against the establishment." Tall, with a head of dark hair, Terry was a good friend and lover. I wanted more of the relationship than he was willing to give during those years in college, so I moved on to other trysts, periodically cycling back to Terry. Later in life, when he found out I was getting married, he sent me this poem:

Today I am blue and I am filled with sadness.
My heart oh so aches and I'm racked with pain.
There once was a woman who loved me so dearly,
But now she is gone and with her the links of our chain.

No one smiled quite like she did.
No one touched me in quite the same way.
No one carried herself quite like she did,
And no one longs quite like me for yesterday.

Now she is happy and this warms my heart,
For deserving she is of the best in this life.
But now I must shed from my mind these old dreams
Of sweet moments together and she as my wife.

I never knew how he felt about me until he sent me this poem three months before my wedding day.

Another guy I would end up with was John, who was also tall and dark-haired. His plans included becoming an ophthalmologist, and he was a great guy. He was rather on the boring side, though, both inside and outside of the bedroom. I was constantly looking for that next edge of excitement. If a person didn't fit the bill, after a while I moved on.

I've often heard of men going around trying to ratchet up the notches on their bedposts with various female conquests. Looking back on the behavior I exhibited, I was like the female counterpart. My sexual exploitations became another symptom of my diseased brain, Glinda. I didn't care if the acquisition was a virgin, dating someone else or even married for that matter. I learned how to manipulate men with flirtation and sex, and it worked well. I also gained pleasure from hurting men emotionally with the impossible goal of getting back at Jeffry. I had no boundaries.

I would do anything to feel good momentarily, including consuming excessive alcohol, engaging in sexual dalliances, and indulging in over or under-eating patterns. Unfortunately, those behaviors that may have made me feel good in the moment would ultimately make me feel worthless over time. I just didn't know how to stop the behavior or break the cycles. I was fighting a battle against an invisible foe, and I was losing.

I was trying to fill a void in my soul by whatever means I could. What I didn't realize was that my superficial lifestyle was causing the chasm to widen and deepen until it became a massive black hole. As in space, black holes consume the dust and gas from the galaxy around them, growing in size. Their gravitational pulls in the galaxies are so strong that even light cannot escape them. Similarly, I was consuming the dirt and filth of my life and creating my own giant black hole—so much so that the beauty and light that was somewhere deep inside could not escape.

CHAPTER 16

NEW ROOMMATES

Our four downstairs roommates found it difficult to study with the location of their bedrooms on the main floor and the constant noise and activity in the Niagara house. They moved out before senior year, so we advertised for four new roommates. Tracy, our other roommate Carrie, and I had the prime real estate upstairs, so we opted to stay in the Niagara house. As luck would have it, four girls from the twin cities in Minnesota, two of which were sisters, were looking for off-campus housing. After meeting us, they decided to move in.

Not knowing the girls previously, we lucked out. Not only were they fun and pretty, but they were wild partiers as well. Perhaps too wild.

We didn't know it then, but when the four moved in, a fifth girl moved in with them. She slept on our couch and her nickname was Mouse. She had her own place to live but must have liked our place better. Most mornings we'd find her passed out on the sofa looking like a sloth on a log.

About five feet tall with blonde, shoulder-length hair and petite in stature, Mouse was a spitfire. She was also quite involved in the drug scene. These five girls loved to party, and before long, our fun-filled party house also became known as a house where drugs were aplenty.

Drugs of all kinds were around us: mushrooms, quaaludes, pot, acid, and cocaine, just to name a few, were stashed downstairs. Four-foot glass bongs and other paraphernalia I didn't even know existed decorated our living room. For me, it felt like living on the top of a keg of dynamite.

Tracy, Carrie, and I—the three upstairs inhabitants—were able to decline involvement in illicit drug partying. We stuck to our legal drug, alcohol, and our weekend binges. As best we could, we tried to overlook and distance ourselves from the illegal downstairs activities.

Any given morning, Mouse would be passed out on our living room davenport, and any number of strange guys would be passed out on the living room floor. Whether it was a weekday or weekend morning, it was anyone's guess what scene we would find upon descending the stairs. We learned to be fully dressed at all times!

One day, one of my roommates, Deb, came home from school looking pale, beat, and deflated. I asked her what was wrong.

"I'm pregnant."

"What?" I asked, unable to comprehend what she was saying.

"I just found out I'm pregnant, and Jim is pissed," Deb said with tears welling up in her eyes and threatening to spill over.

"Oh my God! What are you going to do?" I asked panic inflected in my voice.

"I guess have an abortion. I just went to Student Services and got information on getting one."

Tears now streaming down her face, I embraced her. We rocked back and forth as if she were the child instead of the person with a child beginning to grow inside her body. I told her how sorry I was and cried with her. My tears were for her unborn child, who didn't have a chance because of my roommate's carelessness. For a brief instant, it brought back the pain of my mother's decision long ago, and I cried not only for this child, but for all children not given a chance.

Deb had the abortion. She had two more after that first one. Her sister, Diane, another one of our roommates, also found herself pregnant and had an abortion. The fertile sisters were slow on the learning curve. Diane decided to keep a second pregnancy, and shortly after her senior year in college, she gave birth to a daughter. These consequences seemed like minor hiccups for them, and it didn't slow down their partying ways one little bit.

One weekend night as we were getting ready to go out, Diane asked me to come with her into her back bedroom behind the kitchen. She had something to show me. The dark and chilly room immediately gave me pause as I passed the threshold. It was as if there was a menacing force living inside the room, and I was being halted by an external energy warning me not to advance. A dim light in the corner covered with a red lampshade cast a macabre glow in the room.

My eyes were immediately drawn to the floor, where a round mirror the size of a dinner plate was resting on dark carpet like a round life raft floating in the middle of a darkened sea. Displayed on the mirror were six pencil-thin, white parallel lines that reminded me of soldiers marching along to drill commands.

"What's that?" I asked.

"Cocaine," Diane replied. "I thought you might like to have some with me."

A feeling came over me similar to what I felt that day in the woods when I had my first experience with alcohol ... scared, yet intrigued, by the white stuff. What harm could it do? After all, my roommates had been doing hard drugs all year long, and they seemed to be able to handle it okay school-wise. My mind conveniently forgot all the negative consequences. I was trying to quickly justify what I knew I was about to do.

I looked at Diane to see if she was making a serious offer. After all, I knew cocaine was expensive. Diane smiled and extended her left arm toward the mirrored cocaine, as a game show host would featuring a prize package on *The Price Is Right*.

My eyes shifted to the mirror, as if Jeffry were there hovering as a menacing, yet mesmerizing, face. It felt as if time were suspended. I stared at the mirror while doing battle in my mind. *Should I? Shouldn't I? Should I? Shouldn't I?* After a few seconds, Glinda took hold, and it was as if a light switch turned on. With little hesitancy, I said, "Let's do it!"

Diane produced a rolled-up dollar bill. I didn't have a clue what to do. Feeling as excited as I did before the final school bell rings in June, we sat down on the thick-carpeted floor, and Diane led me through the process of doing a line of cocaine.

It was like diving head-first into an unknown body of water. As I leaned over the mirror, I couldn't believe it was my face looming toward the cocaine. The green eyes staring back at me were the eyes of a person I didn't feel I knew any more.

Mimicking Diane, I inserted the tip of the straw-like dollar bill in my right nostril, holding it with a trembling thumb and forefinger. Closing my other nostril with my left forefinger, I lined up the end of the dollar bill to the left end of a white line. Like reading a line of prose without pause, my fingers made the dollar bill run parallel to the white line as I voraciously vacuumed a line with all the inhalation I could summon. Upon exhalation, I looked at Diane, hoping to receive acclamations for a job well done. With the dollar bill nestled safely in my palm, Diane and I did a high-five in mid-air. Two lines of soldiers down—four to go!

The absorption of cocaine from my mucous membranes into my bloodstream was instant, as if I had been hit with a Taser. Immediately the high was apparent, and it surpassed any buzz from alcohol I had ever experienced. I quickly understood how this white stuff could be addictive.

Diane and I finished off the lines and went out. Invincible and potent after doing the cocaine, we had a grand night of partying. I didn't have the hangover effect of the alcohol the next day. Glinda loved the cocaine. She wanted more. Unfortunately for Glinda, I was a poor college kid and couldn't afford the use of cocaine. Alcohol became my default drug of choice.

CHAPTER 17

JULY 15, 1980

On a hot, midsummer day between junior and senior year, I was getting ready for my first night at work. After pounding the pavement looking for employment, I'd finally been able to secure a cocktail waitress job at Hoffman House, a bar and lounge associated with the Ramada Inn.

The economy was in a recession, so it was especially important for me to earn money. The funds from home supporting my college years were drying up, as the real estate market for Georgia was ebbing. My father was continuing his downward spiral and had recently been fired from his latest job.

My mother informed me that my father had been caught embezzling money from his current employer and school system. His marriage to Boom-boom had only lasted one year. As a college kid, I was caught up in my own life and didn't have much contact with my father anymore. I also tried to limit contact with my mother. I learned the hard way that calling my mother on any given night might result in her remembering the conversation the next day or not. I guess Georgia was coping with life events the only way she knew how—by living in the bottle too.

The heat that summer day—and for many days leading up to this particular afternoon— had been ninety degrees and over, with stifling humidity. I was just thankful to have a job in an air-conditioned building offering respite from the heat.

Donning my uniform, a low V-neck, clingy red miniskirt with a low V-cut back, I pulled black stockings up each leg. Then came the red garter, worn on my right thigh, and a black foot-long, gem-studded feather fastened with a clip in my long hair. Although I felt like a hooker getting ready for a big night out strolling for customers, I had to admit I liked the risqué look in the end. Black, low, patent leather sling-back heels completed the ensemble. I was ready to roll.

It was a reprieve walking into the cool darkness of the Hoffman House from the scorching heat of the day. The tall, dark-haired manager who had hired me showed me around the bar and restaurant. Tom was a serious man who walked like he was chronically constipated and spoke in short retorts only when it was required. His lips only moved the required amount to get the words out before returning to the clenched, thin-lipped pout of a man in lasting pain.

The formality of punching in for the shift and meeting my coworkers took little time, and I was handed my round tray and stacked order pad. I was to shadow Elise, who would be my trainer. Elise was very friendly and in great shape for an older waitress. I guessed her to be in her mid-thirties. She had a small, compact body. Dressed in uniform, she looked like she should be in the Olympic tryouts as a gymnast … minus the feather and garter. She made me feel comfortable and took me around to show me the mechanics of the job.

I was operational before long and working my own tables, with Elise shadowing me. It was a fun job with interesting people. The live entertainment made the atmosphere inviting to the hotel customers. I liked flirting with the suited businessmen, and the flow of alcohol made the environment feel like a second home. If a drink was made incorrectly, Elise and I coerced the bartender to give it to one of us to drink instead of just throwing it out. The perks of the job!

nelly

The bar was a giant "U" shape with the tip of the "U" cordoned off as a station for waitresses to place and gather their drink orders. Glassware hung upside down over the bar like stalactites, the bar-stools positioned under them like targets.

Several hours into my first shift, a new bartender came through the entrance of the "U," the door leading into the bar. He was carrying a cardboard box of bottles I assumed were top-shelf stock for the bar. I was at the waitress station with Elise placing a drink order for a customer.

The bartender's uniform consisted of a white shirt, black bow tie, black vest, and black pants. The new guy's white sleeves were rolled midway up his long arms, and his bulging bicep muscles strained through the upper arms of his shirt as he carried his cargo. He had longer blond hair, which curled to broad shoulders and outlined his darkly tanned and chiseled face.

As he came through the door, he greeted the two other bartenders, Matt and Tom. A quick verbal jab at him by the other bartenders made him smile and chuckle. White, straight teeth lit up his face. His wide shoulders and tapered waist bent over and placed the box of alcohol on the floor. He disappeared momentarily behind the bar, and I reflexively held my breath until he reappeared.

At the same time that I saw this Adonis-like man, a loud thunderstorm was brewing outside. Near the stage where the band was setting up to play was a door leading directly to the outside parking lot, presumably for ease in carrying in band equipment. Someone had left the door completely propped open.

As the entire bar and wait staff peered out to where the intensifying storm originated, a lightning bolt visibly struck a metal pole in the outside parking lot. Inside, you could feel the sizzle of electricity meeting metal. I knew just how that pole felt—Adonis-man had done the same to my heart. I flashed back to how my grandfather must have felt atop the train when he was struck by lightning. History was repeating itself.

"Who is that?" I asked Elise, my head gesturing toward Adonis-man as my arms hugged my drink tray.

"That's Michael," she responded in a breathy sigh.

"Wow, he's a doll!" I said under my own breath. With the noise in the bar, Elise never heard me ... or she chose to ignore my comment.

"Back to work!" Elise stated as one of the bartenders delivered our drink order. We both snapped out of the momentary weather and hormonal diversions. I loaded the drink order on my tray, but my only thought was that I couldn't wait to drink-in the sight of Michael again. My heart began to ache from the aftershock of the metaphoric lightning strike as I forced myself to turn from the bar and sashay away.

As the night progressed, the storm outside continued. Hundred mile-an-hour horizontal winds and rain were being reported outside. Trees and power lines were down throughout the county. I could hear warning sirens in the distance, even over the din of the bar and musical entertainment. Local travel warnings were communicated before television stations lost broadcasting capabilities.

Tom, the constipated manager, was running around like a nervous new father waiting for the birth of his child. He had the brilliant idea of serving free drinks in the bar to wait out the storm. The bar started to become packed with stranded outsiders and hotel guests. It was like a free-for-all inside the lounge. Had the storm progressed to a tornadic level of destruction at Hoffman House, we would have been impaled by the amount of glassware in the lounge.

Being on my feet all night, I had developed blisters from breaking in my new pumps. Deciding I'd had enough of this chaotic scene, I turned my attention to Michael. Sitting down at the end of the bar where he was stationed, I started conversing with him as he was rustling up drinks as fast as he could.

In the midst of the storm and bar turmoil, Michael and I intermittently chatted and flirted. There was an immediate palpable magnetic pull between us. Michael was like a hummingbird flitting back and forth behind the bar—I, the flower, perched on the bar stool. After serving drinks, he would come back and talk to me, making sure I was doing okay before quickly flying away to another call of duty.

Through bits and pieces of information, I learned that Michael had been in bar and restaurant management after high school. He'd moved around the country after high school opening Ramada Inns, but had recently decided to come back to his home town, Eau Claire, to pursue a college degree in business.

He felt distressed about the scene in front of us. The last thing he thought we should be doing was serving free drinks to people and then letting them get into cars to drive through downed trees and live power lines.

The storm finally abated, and I was able ... by the grace of God ... to make it home safely that night. I'm not sure how I managed to get home to the little grey house on Niagara Street, other than I was flying high on the adrenaline of the first night at work, the effects of a raging storm, and my time with Michael. When I pulled up to the curb, I noticed that our house was black. There wasn't a light on anywhere in the block. We had no electricity. Entering the house, I found several of my roommates huddled together on the couch over candlelight. They were all abuzz from the afterglow of the storm.

The next day, a couple of my roommates and I went driving around. I'd actually have to zigzag down unfamiliar streets, because everywhere I turned there were huge trees ripped out of the ground and toppled over crushed cars or blocking streets completely. Power lines were hanging like broken tightropes. Shattered glass sprinkled the ground in front of storefronts, making a magical carpeted entrance to open stores, welcoming potential looters. Roofs were blown off houses, and old barns that had withstood the test of time lay in heaps of rubble.

Twenty-four thousand trees were lost that night. One person died when a refrigerator fell on her in her trailer home. In trailer parks, the aluminum houses were flipped 180 degrees, looking like dogs beckoning a belly rub. There were several injuries and over 160 million dollars in damage. On Niagara Street, we were without power for seven days. It was the storm of the century in Eau Claire. T-shirts were immediately produced that said "I survived July 15, 1980."

I fell in love with Michael that night. As my roommates and I were nestled on the couch over candlelight, I announced I had met the man I was going to marry. It was a vision that eventually came true. Little did I know that meeting my future husband on such a stormy night would be a foreshadowing of things to come.

CHAPTER 18

GRANDMA

I got dressed in a pair of black slacks and a red sweater, attempting to look nice and professional for my nursing presentation later in the morning. Out of a class of ninety-two students, I was one of the last ones scheduled to give a speech for the entire nursing class and faculty.

The phone rang and one of my roommates yelled up the stairs, "Nelly, for you. I think it's your mom!"

I grabbed the receiver out of its cradle at the top of the stairs and in a short, rushed tone said, "Hello?"

"Hi, honey, it's Mom. I have some bad news. Your ... grandma ... passed away ... this morning." Quickened sobs separated the words.

"Oh no!" I said. "I'm so sorry, Mom." After an uncomfortable silence, I asked, "Didn't you know I had a big presentation this morning? And you decided to tell me now? I'm running late; I'll call you later, okay?"

"Sure, I just thought you would want to know."

"Thanks, Mom. I really have to run."

Walking down the hill to the nursing building, I began to feel guilty about cutting off my mother on the phone. Memories of what a great woman and grandmother I'd lost flashed through my thoughts.

Grandma had been diagnosed with Bell's palsy, which affected her muscles. Six months into her eightieth year of life, her facial muscles had begun drooping. Shortly after that, my mother would find butter stored in the oven, or the coffee pot put in the freezer. Although Bell's palsy wasn't life threatening, it marked the beginning of her deteriorating health, declining mental status, and eventual dying process.

The last time I'd seen my grandmother was at her nursing home near our house. She had resided there for only a few months. As far as nursing homes go, this one was okay. My mother and I had entered Grandma's room, and she just stared at us with vacant, unknowing, robin-shell blue eyes. As we entered the room, she tried to say something, but words came out garbled, like she was speaking with a mouth full of marbles.

She pointed to her commode near the bed, so my mother went out to get a nursing assistant to help. My grandmother reached out her arms to me, and I knew instinctively she needed me to get her on her commode quickly. As fast as I could, I moved her commode next to the bed and locked the wheels, putting up the toilet seat. I reached for my grandmother and her outstretched arms and instructed her to swivel to a seated position on the end of the bed, feet firmly on the floor. I then told her to stand and I would get her to the potty. As she stood and I struggled to hang on to her and get her undergarments down, loose stool and urine ran down both legs.

My mother walked in at that moment with a nursing assistant. "Oh my God!" she exclaimed, covering her mouth with her hand and running out of the room in tears.

"Shut the door," I said calmly to the nursing assistant standing like a statue near the door. "We need to get her cleaned up."

Even though my grandma probably didn't know what had happened, nor could she verbalize her disgust at the situation, I saw tears in her rheumy eyes.

I smiled lovingly at her and patted her age-spotted, veined hand. "I bet you feel better now, don't you, Grandma? You did a great job! We'll just need to clean you up a bit, and then you can go back to bed, okay?"

No response.

My grandma was a grand lady—gracious, loving, and refined. At the end of her life, she was reduced to an infantile state, at least physically. I hope she knew I'd treated her with all the loving respect she deserved. She didn't live long after that visit.

I strutted with purpose down the aisle at the nursing auditorium. I said a quick prayer and asked my grandma to help me out.

Standing next to the overhead projector, I assembled my notes and the clear overhead sheets I would be using as information. My reflection on my grandmother made me feel morose, and I wanted to run out of the theater in a fit of tears, similar to Georgia that day in the nursing home. I didn't think that would be acceptable to the stodgy, nun-like professors sitting in the arena, so I took a deep breath and began.

Lights dimmed, overhead projector on, I cleared my throat. It was go time!

"My presentation today is entitled 'Teaching Relaxation Techniques for the Elderly Population.' The elderly population is at risk for increasing stressors due to … there are many techniques we can use as nurses to aid this population … some of the proven techniques used are muscle relaxation, visualization …"

POP! An audible sound and complete darkness surrounded me. There was no longer an overhead projector lit up. The bulb had burned out. I fiddled with the on/off switch, hoping for a miraculous luminosity, all too aware that I had several more overheads to use in my speech, and several minutes left of lecture material. Someone responsible for lights turned the auditorium lights up a bit brighter, and I did the only thing I could think of at that moment—I continued on, pretending the projector was still on and that everyone could see what I was presenting. I finished my pontification.

After all the class assignments were done for the day, one of the nursing instructors came up to me and said, "You did exactly the right thing by continuing with your demonstration. That showed us you have good control in a stressful situation."

I thanked her, got a grin on my face, and said in a matter of fact manner, "I know. I just found out this morning my grandma died. We were very close." The nursing instructor looked horrified, sympathetic, and questioning all at the same time. Her chin dropped, and her mouth formed an "O," but no words came out of the hole.

"Grandma did that with the projector as a way to come and say goodbye to me," I clarified.

"Oh," she replied, head bent and shuffling quickly down the hall, with her rubber soled shoes squeaking as she went. I received an "A" on that exercise.

As the years wore on, I would have a chance to call upon Grandma's spirit to guide and help me through some of my darkest hours. She has always been there for me alive or dead, which is more than I could say for her daughter—my mother, Georgia.

CHAPTER 19

MICHAEL-PART 1

Michael never got to meet my grandma before she died. We began dating shortly after the July 15 storm. I fell madly in love with Michael. It was an intense attraction. We both liked drinking and partying, and got along very well.

It began one night after the bar closed at Hoffman House. Michael invited me back to his apartment. We drove up to a two-story white house on a tree-lined residential street called Babcock Street.

"This is a cute house, Michael," I said, somewhat surprised by the ordinary nature of where he lived.

"Thanks, my apartment is on the bottom, and I live here with three old ladies each in their own apartments. They are nice and quiet. I think they like me living here, because I shovel the sidewalk for them in the winter and help carry up their groceries when I'm around."

"That's really nice of you. I bet they love having you here," I replied, thinking what a caring guy Michael was.

On the left side of the house were an eight-by-ten concrete slab and the entrance to his apartment. Inside you climbed up five steps to face a wall. To the right was a small, neutral-colored living room with windows that allowed natural light to enter during the day. In the right corner was a fish tank where several Oscars were swimming lazily in the water, with colorful rocks on the bottom and a backdrop of tropical lush, green scenery. The quiet bubbling and aeration of the pump, along with the subtle tank light, gave a relaxed humming sound to the now-darkened room.

In the opposite corner of the room stood an upside down black bicycle, balanced by handlebars, with the seat resting on the green carpet. The back tire was off the bike and resting against the nearby wall. Chains for various gears hung like a necklace around the kickstand. Behind the bike was another door that Michael explained led out to the house's main hallway and front door. The old ladies used the hallway to get to their apartments, and at the top of the stairs was a community bathroom shared by the women.

Michael's living room housed a long, black and brown striped off-white couch. A beat up rocking chair covered by an old army blanket, and a television hoisted to eye level by several milk crates, finished the furnishings. With the door removed from the living room closet, there was enough room on several adjustable shelves to house a quality stereo component system as well. Michael adeptly punched several buttons and turned various knobs, and soft music floated in waves across the room.

Leaving the living room, we retreated past the entry stairs to enter a small compact kitchen, which upon flipping the light switch became bright, sunny yellow and glossy white. The smell of turpentine hung in the air, and the walls and cabinetry contrasted an old, tile-weathered floor. Clearly the room held a layer of fresh paint. An old gas burning stove, like something you would see at Grandma's house, graced the room. The kitchen was cheery and reminded me of sunshine.

Looking around, I spied two pictures on the refrigerator. One was of a beautiful, dark- haired girl with a broad grin of straight, white teeth and wearing a patchwork quilted shirt. Her green eyes sparkled at the camera lens. The second picture was that of a little dark-haired boy about seven years old. There was a note next to the boy's picture that read: "Michael, I really like the people here, and especially you. You seem a lot like me, and I hope I grow up to be like you! Your buddy, Rob."

With a twinge low in my belly, I asked Michael if the picture of the girl was his girlfriend.

"No," he replied. "That's a high school friend who lived here before me. I got this apartment because she decided to move out."

I asked about the little boy.

"He's a kid I met while living in Madison in another apartment."

This guy is not only gorgeous, but old ladies and young kids love him. What a guy!

Beyond the quaint little kitchen was a tiny bedroom that could house a double bed but not much more. The closet was the size of a broom closet. Clothes were packed in like sardines in a can. Sleeves of shirts were a tangled mess and unidentifiable garment items hung half in and half out of the closet, like they couldn't decide whether to come or go.

"This is a really cute and cozy apartment, but where is the bathroom you use?" I asked, feeling the urge to utilize the facilities.

"Well, that depends," he said. "You can use the bathroom up the front stairs. The one the old ladies share. Or you can use mine, but it's downstairs in the basement."

"I can use yours if you want to show me the basement," I said without hesitation.

"Okay," he said "You asked for it!"

We took a right by the entryway stairs and descended into the bowels of the house. A large, grey furnace was rumbling and making choking noises in the corner. The ceilings were low, and there were round, octopus-silver arms extending overhead from the furnace to blow warm air up to the apartments. The furnace and apparatus looked like a giant Tin Man with multiple extremities reaching out in a sea above us.

"You should see this place in the winter," Michael said. "It's the warmest place in Eau Claire. The old ladies are constantly cold, so they crank up the heat. I'm the first one these arms deliver the heat to, so I usually have the windows open all winter long, since I don't have to pay for heat."

"How much is rent at a place like this?" I asked.

"I pay seventy-five dollars a month with heat included," Michael replied.

"Wow! That's the cheapest rent I ever heard of!" I exclaimed.

We progressed under the Tin Man arms toward the back of the house, coming upon a bathroom that housed a commode. When standing at the toilet, another step forward would land you in the stand-up shower the size of Michael's bedroom closet. A piece of green and brown shag carpet was thrown on the floor in attempt to carpet the cement slab. The air was moist and steamy.

"There you go! I'll wait upstairs for you," Michael said as he turned away from me and retreated toward the stairs.

"Thanks a lot," I muttered under my breath. As I advanced toward the porcelain bowl, I saw bluish-grey, shiny silverfish scurrying around the edges of the carpet. I'm sure they loved the heat and humidity the bathroom provided. I was afraid if I lifted the lip of the carpet, I would find a silverfish condo—living at its finest! I was gaining a picture of why this apartment's rent was so cheap.

Climbing the steps to the apartment, I kept expecting the Tin Man furnace to come alive, or the bogeyman to jump out from the muted shadows of the basement. For a brief moment, I wondered what I had gotten myself into.

Our relationship quickly advanced to an intimate sexual one, but we also spent a significant amount of time hanging out and enjoyed each other's company. Michael was my opposite—laid back, spontaneous, and exciting. I was more serious and focused, with my life goals planned. We complemented each other well.

nelly

I spent a lot of time at that apartment on Babcock Street. Grocery shopping and running over to make Michael breakfast or a home-cooked meal at night after he was done working became a habit. Many nights we spent talking into the wee hours of the morning. Being with Michael in that little apartment on Babcock Street felt like home.

One day, Michael and his brother came home as I was nestled into the daisy-like kitchen baking cookies. Michael's younger brother Jonathon, or Jon, was a slimmer, less polished, scruffier version of Michael. His teeth were crooked as well as cigarette-stained, and it distracted from his overall appearance as soon as he opened his mouth. Michael's brother also had a triangular shaped scarred patch on his skin poking out above his blue plaid button down shirt. The stretched, mottled skin was left as a reminder of an earlier tragedy. As a fire's flame would leap upward from a candle, his skin scar was tapered at the top like a flush-colored flame flirting with licking his face. When Jonathon went shirtless, the scarring covered most of his front torso.

Michael had told me the story about Jon's accident as a teenager. Jon was at a bonfire one Friday night drinking and partying, and a buddy of his threw gasoline on the active fire pit. The fire leapt at Jon, devouring him with its flames. Jon teetered between life and death but came out on top, with multiple areas of burn tissue as a skin tapestry to tell the story. Looking at the extent of the fire damage, I knew the pain must have been unbearable. No one really talked about that incident in Michael's family.

Besides the two men, there were two blondish-red, furry four-legged puppies with them. The puppies came around the corner and into the kitchen, pushing and shoving each other and getting tangled up in long legs and unsure footing like only puppies can do. Their tongues were lolling out the sides of their mouths, and they were panting with excitement as I bent down to embrace their playful charging.

"Oh my God, how cute are they!" I looked up at Michael with adoring eyes as I scooped them both in my arms.

"Meet Atty and Cody, our new dogs. We just went and picked them up in Cadott. They're sisters and were free," Michael announced. "So Jon and I each got one."

"But you aren't supposed to have pets here, Michael," I said, spoiling the moment as the pups licked my face and squirmed in my arms.

"We'll just keep it from the landlord. John never comes around here much, anyway. It'll be fine," Michael said convincingly.

"They are so cute and adorable," I mumbled, still getting full puppy breath and a tongue bath all over my face.

Some of the best moments of our lives came from having that dog; Atty. Atty is short for Attitude. Michael always wanted a dog he could call and say, "good Attitude/bad Attitude." She was a great Golden Retriever mutt and loved chasing Frisbees and swimming. You could tell Atty to "stay" and she wouldn't move a muscle off that cement slab on the side of the house. She would rather die than have an accident in the apartment, but boy did she like to destroy things! Whole arms of chairs were demolished. Calculators, school books, glasses, remotes … anything she could see she would chew and destroy when we were gone. But we loved her unconditionally, and she loved us. We were a family of three.

Between work and school, Atty became our entertainment during time off—taking her to Carson Park to swim in shallow pools of water; bringing a little Weber grill and having a picnic of roasted chicken and a six pack of Bud, or whatever beer was on sale. We thought we were living large. Some days I look back on those simple times as the best memories of all. We were dirt poor, in love, and just kids trying to figure out life.

Often Jon, Cody, Michael, Atty, and I would horse around together. One evening at dusk about a year after Jon and Michael had brought the dog's home, Jon drove into the driveway. I could tell by the way he was walking toward the house—stooped over, eyes to the ground—that something was wrong. As he entered the apartment, Michael joked around with him.

"Someone die? You look like you just came from a funeral."

Jon looked up at the both of us with misty eyes and said, "Cody got hit by a car and is dead. We have to go up to Mom and Dad's and bury her."

We all went up to Michaels' parents' house to dig a grave large enough to house Atty's 150-pound sister. She was in good company there, though. It was like a pet cemetery in back of Michael's house: Toonie, Muffy, Chloe, Kugels, and many more mutts were buried in the back yard of that old farmhouse.

After burying Cody and saying our goodbyes to Michael's parents, we got in the car to leave. Jon, sitting in the back seat, decided now would be a great time for us all to do a couple of lines of cocaine he had gotten from a friend, so the three of us indulged in that magical white powder. The hurt over losing the dog turned into chemical relief, and Glinda was once again happy.

CHAPTER 20

MICHAEL-PART 2

The first time I met Michael's entire family, he told me to dress in old jeans and a T-shirt. He picked me up early on a Saturday morning in his baby blue Chevy, and we traveled up Clairemont Avenue toward Cameron Street. Turning right on Cameron, we rode past small single family houses with exteriors and yards kept in pristine shape intermixed with what looked to be rental-type duplexes.

The front yards of the duplexes had bikes and various children's toys strewn across the front yards, making them look like junkyards next to the quaint family dwellings. We drove several blocks and then turned left into a narrow, graveled, circular drive. The annular drive cut along the back of a white, two-story farmhouse with a large cement front porch.

The stoop made the house looks inviting, with baskets of vibrant red impatiens hanging along the perimeter, and a couple of rocking chairs nestled in the shade next to the house. Michael parked the Chevy in back of a line of several pickup trucks, both new and old. Ladders, paint cans, and various pieces of equipment littered the back of the house, and crushed beer cans were scattered about the lawn like sprinkles on a birthday cake.

nelly

Michael explained to me during the drive that as he grew up, theirs was the only house "out in the country," and only within the past few decades had the town of Eau Claire "spread out this way." He relayed how he would have to hitchhike into town for any high school activities, since his parents never drove the kids anywhere. He didn't tell me much else about his family, simply saying, "You'll just have to meet them." I was nervous meeting them for the first time, but he assured me with a chuckle that I would have nothing to worry about, so I should just relax.

Once out of the car, Michael led the way, entering the house from a back screen door. We passed through a small, musty smelling entryway that stored large roasting pans, silver pots, and rarely used kitchen appliances like food shredders and canning equipment. Mason jars lined up along metal shelving like glass soldiers with tin top hats.

I heard loud, booming male voices sparring and deep laughter emanating from somewhere near the core of the house. It was so loud and raucous; it made me want to retreat back to the solitude of the back yard. Michael was generally soft-spoken, reserved, and more aloof. We angled through a half-bath off the kitchen and entered a large country kitchen where the people attached to the voices congregated.

"About time you guys got here," a blaring, deep voice bellowed at us.

No one was introduced to me. I was handed a can of cold Bud Light and a paintbrush and told "daylight's a burnin', girl!" Five other people our age had their painting supplies and beer already in hand, and they started filing out the kitchen door in single file.

Michael's dad sat down with a heavy thud into a large, desk-like chair housed at a round Formica kitchen table. It was 9:00 a.m. He cracked open his own Bud Light, sending a fine mist of beer airborne. At the same time, he waved his hand toward us in dismissal and hollered, "Get going now!" Michael and I left the kitchen as ordered, the screen door slamming in our wake.

Although I wasn't accustomed to cracking a beer right after breakfast, I had to admit that as we began our assigned task of painting the exterior of the farmhouse, and the day warmed, the beer went down easy and tasted pretty good. Throughout the day, I met and enjoyed the company of the other cheap laborers. They were Michael's brother, Mark, and his girlfriend, Jenny; brother Jonathon and his girlfriend, Belinda; and his sister, Jane. In birth order, it went Mark, Jane, Michael, and Jonathon. His parents were James and Dot.

Michael's dad, Jim, was a blue-collar worker and plumber by trade. He stood five feet ten and had a military buzz cut and sizable beer belly. As Michael informed me: "My dad is an opinionated son of a bitch!" Growing up, Michael despised his father. Jim would rip the phone off the wall in the kitchen if it rang after 8:00 p.m. He'd take his belt to the kids if they so much as fidgeted or snickered in church Sunday morning. On rare family outings, Jim would sit in the family auto with engine running, laying on the horn, and hollering at Dot to get the kids and all their belongings gathered into the car ... "Now!"

Any topic of conversation with Jim would turn into "the government is a bunch of corrupt assholes, just out to line their own pockets." Schools and teachers "didn't know anything, and are teaching garbage these days." Doctors were "only out to get richer" and "put you on pills you don't really need." The only good institutions in Jim's opinion were "the union" that protected workers' rights, and the "VFW," where he and Dot historically chose to carouse mid-day like clockwork rather than raise and nurture their own brood.

Jim was a bigoted redneck, but he was clever. He was always trying to figure out how to get something for nothing. Somehow, he tapped into the city water system and never paid a penny. He would have the greenest lawn on Cameron Street during drought-like summers. No one was the wiser. He would splice into cable and get television channels free. Over the twenty plus years I knew Jim; he worked a total of three years. Somehow, he got health insurance for life off those minimal years of labor. I don't know how he did it, but he was really good at manipulating the "system," and benefited greatly by doing so. He also believed he was entitled to such liberties.

nelly

I instantly liked Dot, Michael's mother. She stood ram-rod straight at five-seven in height. She had short, curly, brown hair and wore wire-rimmed glasses. She had a box-like figure after birthing four children. If you took measurements around her breasts, abdomen, and hips, they would come out to be the same number. She walked with a slight limp because of a bad knee, but looked younger than her forty-eight years.

Once Dot found out that I was a nursing student, I became like a daughter to her. Her aspiration growing up had been to become a nurse, but Jim had come along as a young, uniformed man and swept her off her feet before she could fulfill that dream. She giggled as she talked about meeting Jim, and would say coquettishly, "I got picked up in a pickup truck and that was that!" After four years of marriage, the children came one after another, and her fate as a stay-at-home mom was sealed.

Mark was a mini-me of his father—outspoken, opinionated, and loud. He was a replica of Jim, and hence went into the plumbing profession. He had dated his girlfriend, Jenny, since high school. They eventually married. She was short, heavier set at times, and always wore high heels. Jenny was a laid back and happy spirit. She put up with Mark's strident nature, and thus they made a balanced couple. Jenny would roll her eyes and shrug as Mark and Jim got into a heated debate about the deteriorating state of city, state, and country.

Jane was a pretty girl and had the closest relationship to Michael. She had long, straight, blonde hair, was five-five in height, and had a good figure. She welcomed me into the family as a sister would. She also liked her beer a bit too much. Her nickname was "more malt Mable," but she had a heart of gold and would give anything she had to anyone in need. She had the brain power like Michael, but decided not to go to college. She worked in the office on the railroad and seemed intermittently content.

Jonathon was the baby of the family and came four years after Michael. He was generally a loose cannon. He ran with a tough crowd and liked to get into bar fights and brawls. He tended to hang around petty thieves and individuals with drug connections. He, like Jim, was always looking for the next scam or way to beat the system. When Jonathon was in a rare moment of sobriety, he was a thoughtful, caring soul.

As time passed, we would spend holidays at Michael's house. One Christmas we had saved up a significant amount of loose change to play our usual round of cards. With holiday cheer, everyone was seated at the kitchen table, coupled with their alcoholic drink of choice. Anteing up dimes or quarters, the family played rounds of poker or "in-between." There was a small, garishly decorated, fiber-optic Christmas tree alternating vibrant seasonal colors in the living room within view. Glittering fiber-optic Santa's and elves were on the kitchen countertops and stove. We were surrounded by waves of color and holiday potpourri candle fragrances as we settled into the seriousness of winning money at cards.

During the first few hours of frivolity, everyone seemed to be having fun. As is common in families, the conversation turned to "growing up" years. Jane at one point said, "We had a rotten childhood. You two were in the bar every afternoon, so we basically had to raise ourselves!"

"It wasn't that bad. You had a roof over your head, and plenty of food on the table," piped in Jim.

All the kids snorted and rolled their eyes. Michael continued on memory lane.

"The only good memory I have growing up is putting up Christmas lights outside. We had the big old-fashioned bulbs, and our house would light up like an airport runway!"

"Yeah, but half the time we didn't have mittens or warm coats, so we ended up freezing, which would ruin the night. You, Michael, would have to wear my hand-me-downs, because you didn't get anything for yourself," added Jane.

"Don't remind me!" Michael said with sarcasm in his voice. Yet when I looked into his baby blues, I saw hurt gathering right below the surface. I couldn't imagine a macho guy like Michael having to wear girls' hand-me-downs, let alone run around the neighborhood in them.

Jonathon, looking wall-eyed after consuming a half case of beer over the previous hours, had been listening to the banter but had remained silent in his brooding. All of the sudden, like flipping on a light switch, Jonathon jumped out of his seat, jolting the kitchen table and toppling his chair. Cards, money, and alcohol went flying around the kitchen as some of us instinctively hopped away from the epicenter. Jonathon bulldozed across the room toward Jim, towering over his still-seated father. He wrapped his hands around Jim's massive neck, attempting to choke the life out of him. Jonathon shouted all sorts of obscenities at his father, saying that he was the "worst piece of shit" he'd ever known.

Then, as if on cue, Jane decided to join the fray and went after her mother, trying to throttle her while shouting about what a horrible mother she had been. Mark went after Jonathon and pulled him off their dad. Michael wrangled Jane off their mom. I managed to end up curled in a ball on the kitchen floor, sobbing and pleading for the chaos to stop.

Jonathon stood lean and tall and began a tirade about the injustices caused by his parents. Most of what he was spewing was unintelligible snippets of words or phrases. He stood in the middle of the kitchen, unzipped his pants, and pulled out his penis, shaking the flaccid appendage. He said in a crystal-clear voice: "Anyone want some of this?" His laser vision of hostility was aimed toward his father. Jim's massive frame stood, face engorged and reddened. With spittle flying, Jim pointed to the door.

"Get the hell out of here!" he raged. "What is *wrong* with you?"

Jonathon, like he was coming out of a trance, looked around the room at the bedlam he'd initiated. Like a balloon quickly deflating, tears began streaming down his sunken face.

Nelly Branson

"Fuck you," he said in a hushed voice to no one in particular. He attempted to put his penis back into his pants, swaying on unsteady feet as he tried to zip up. It took several tries to contain himself, and everyone sat staring, their mouths agape. Leaving his coat behind, Jonathon stormed past my perch on the floor and exited the kitchen into the dark night. The door slammed shut, making his flight the final exclamation point to the pandemonium. We could hear more muffled discord as Jonathon seemed to get a resurgence of rage on his way from the porch to his car.

In the aftermath inside the house, we looked at one another in disbelief and took a collective sigh as we righted furniture and picked up drinks. As quickly as the atmosphere became subdued, we heard a crash as glass shattered. Some of us ran to the window to find out what had happened and saw Jonathon standing in the moonlit backdrop of the cold night, staring as if mystified at his right fist. Even from a distance we could see blood running down his hand in concert with the falling snowflakes, making a rapidly expanding dark red pool against the white ground at his feet. An anger-fueled strike, he had slammed his fist through the driver's side window of his car, splintering it into shards. That Christmas night, Michael's mom and I ended up taking Jonathon to the hospital where I worked to have his severed hand and wrist tended. After hearing the cause of the injury, the hospital personnel tried to get Michael's mom to sign commitment papers or sign for a seventy-two-hour mental health hold at the very least. Nervously biting her nails, Dot mutely and slowly shook her head, refusing to institutionalize and help her youngest child.

During our time at the hospital, Jonathon paced around the emergency department in the standard blue and white hospital gown, backside flapping open in his wake. His left unbandaged hand held desperately onto the rolling IV pole to provide steadiness to his gait. Clear bags of normal saline dangled with attached tubing in Jonathon's arm, trying to replace lost blood volume. Jonathon jerked the pole around the emergency department, IV bags shifting back and forth like a fish flopping on a dock. He was mumbling incoherently at the stand and having what appeared to be a one-way conversation with his IV bag. It was heartbreaking to watch this deranged, sick, young man.

Perhaps the strangest part of the night was how comfortable I felt in the surrounding turmoil. As I sat in that emergency room, I thought to myself, *here's to another Merry Fucking Christmas!*

Several years later, Jonathon would accuse Michael's dad of molesting him as a child. I never believed Jonathon. Michael did.

CHAPTER 21

TOGETHER

Three years into our relationship, the night with Dr. Joe happened. Neither Joe nor I pressed charges against Michael. Before I saw Michael again, a letter showed up under my door. It read:

> For the last couple of days, I have done a tremendous amount of soul searching. In that time, I have answered many questions, but more are left unsolved.

> Once I told you I was afraid to lose my temper. I said and did things that I will be ashamed of the rest of my life. Anger and rage were out of control. Thank God Joe was able to get out. I might have hurt him seriously.

> A problem throughout our relationship was my immaturity toward showing affection and love. It was not by accident this happened. I felt that if I didn't get too close, you would never be hurt if I didn't measure up to the standards two people in

love must have. Many times I could see you're hurt and did nothing. I am so sorry.

Please try to understand that you will never know how good you have had something until you have lost it. You never hurt me; you sacrificed everything. A day wouldn't go by where I wasn't feeling like an asshole; the more you gave just made it harder on the both of us …

Well, you have made your decision. How could I have ever known how hurt I would be? Do you know what I keep saying to myself? I wish I could change the past. I wish all of this would have never happened.

I believe love is made of many emotions, and you cannot truly love someone until you feel as if your heart is going to break without that special person. You tried to make every day happy, simple, and undemanding. You should have made me make some sacrifices. I took your love, enjoyed it, used it, and after a while become numb toward it. I hurt you too much, and the scars became worse. At times, I wished you would do something wrong so I could hurt. So I could see how much you meant to me. It would have helped me see clearly.

My father says, "There isn't anything that can happen that is so bad that something good can't come out of it." He is right. I've learned, I've lost, I hurt so bad inside, and now I can change. If this wouldn't have happened, I don't know how much longer I could have gone on with such a bad attitude about trust, honesty, love, and devotion.

If the damage is irreversible, if you choose to find another, if I have lost you forever, please remember that tomorrow is another day—we can grow with it.

Love, Michael

P.S. Sorry about the door.

After receiving this letter and visiting Michael at his apartment, I moved in with him to live in the little apartment on Babcock Street. We were committed to one another, and Michael finished college three years later with a degree in business finance. Waiting for Michael to finish school, I entered graduate school and took a full graduate load while continuing to work full-time on the oncology unit at the hospital.

Sitting in that bright, sunny kitchen one day after Michael's graduation, I said to him, "It's been six years of dating, with three of those living together. We need to make plans to get married or I need to move on."

We started making plans to get married, and on August 9, 1986, we got married at Hope Lutheran Church in Eau Claire, WI. Not only did we get married that day, but I graduated on the same day with my master's degree in Nursing Administration. Needless to say, I didn't attend my graduation ceremony.

My favorite uncle, a Lutheran minister, officiated at our wedding. Prior to getting married, as all young couples do, we had to undergo pre-marital counseling sessions. Since we weren't members of Hope Lutheran, we were required to receive that counseling from the church pastor. I don't remember his name, but he interviewed us individually and found that we were similar in terms of our life goals, values, desire for children, and outlook on finances—in all the major things couples shared, he found us compatible.

After a few sessions of one-on-one counseling, we were required to take a 125- question written test for a more detailed analysis of our compatibility. After taking the test, we were called into the pastor's office. He looked at us very seriously and said, "I don't know how to tell you this, but I don't think this marriage will last."

Michael and I looked at each other questioningly as the pastor continued. "You answered on the opposite spectrum for all major areas of the test. For example, Nelly replied being completely comfortable naked in front of you, Michael, but you don't seem to feel comfortable being naked in front of her." The pastor looked dubiously at Michael.

"Well, that is pretty weird, since I run around naked in front of Nelly all the time," Michael responded. After further exploration of the responses on the test, we discovered that Michael had answered the scale in reverse on every question. The scale ran 1–5; from strongly disagree to strongly agree. He read the scale as strongly agree to strongly disagree, so he answered each question the polar opposite of how he felt.

After unearthing this revelation, the minister looked at us and said, "Well, you two are good to go then. You scared me for a second!"

I looked at the minister square in his bloodshot, weary eyes and said, "I have a feeling my life with Michael won't be boring."

Other than my car not starting the morning of the wedding because of a dead battery, and a light rain mid-afternoon, it was a wonderful day. The sun came out to shine brightly upon us and at 3:00 p.m., and on August 9th, 1986; we began our life as husband and wife.

Some people attended the ceremony more out of curiosity than love for us. There was mention of "selling front row seats" to the occasion. Since my divorced parents were seeing each other for the first time in years and Michael's volatile family dynamics were well known, some people were anticipating it could be quite a show.

For our sake, everyone behaved during the wedding. The next day at gift opening, Georgia inexplicably threw a tantrum and stormed out of Michael's house!

CHAPTER 22
BEGINNING MARRIAGE

As predicted, our first eight years of marriage was filled with twists and turns. Michael began his career as a stockbroker for E.F. Hutton. He made cold calls to potential clients and made money by selling securities and other financial products. Michael earned a negligible salary. He spent a fair amount of time in bars most nights after work, "entertaining" potential clients and schmoozing with other brokers. All in the name of advancing his client base.

On October 19, 1987, Michael pulled his tan station wagon slowly into our driveway. As he stepped out of the car in his tailored suit and lacquered dress shoes, his broad shoulders drooped, as if touching the ground would be a welcomed relief. He entered the house we were renting, and instead of the usual broad smile and hug, I received a verbal, dismissive "harrumph."

The dog, sensing his master's low spirits, tucked her fanned tail between her hind legs. Atty and I followed Michael down the hallway, which appeared to darken along with his mood.

"What on earth happened? You look like someone died."

"Haven't you watched the news today?" Michael stated in a resigned fashion.

"No, I've been busy all day. What happened?" Insistence echoed in my voice.

"The stock market crashed. Dow Jones dropped over 500 points today. They're calling it Black Monday. The experts are comparing today's drop to the stock market crash of 1929. I've been on the phone all day talking to clients and telling them their life savings have virtually vaporized. Everyone's in a panic."

Me, being the eternal optimist … or maybe it was my stupidity in anything dealing with investment concepts … said, "Well, how bad can it be? Won't it turn around? You always say to invest for the long haul!"

Michael looked at me with a measure of disdain and idiocy.

"You don't understand," his voice escalated. "People are threatening to sue me and E.F. Hutton, or even worse … commit suicide! These are peoples' livelihoods and futures at stake! It's like a fucking nightmare! Just my luck to become a stockbroker right before a historic crash," he mumbled in a softer, resigned tone.

After graduating with my master's degree, I began my first nursing administrative job. I became the director of nursing for a small forty-bed rural hospital attached to 120-bed nursing home south of Eau Claire.

The job was intense. On any given day, I could be dealing with staffing issues, physician requests, budget constraints, supply orders, labor and delivery, or an ambulance run to Eau Claire due to a farmer losing his leg in a combine tractor accident. I enjoyed the variety the job offered, but it was extremely challenging and demanding. I put in long hours and barely saw my husband.

After being there a year, I received a devastating phone call. It was a cold, blizzard-filled winter morning at 4:00 a.m. Becky, my second in command at the hospital, called and said in a calm, steady voice, "I just wanted to let you know that there was a car accident last night. Two of the staff was killed, and I didn't want you hearing about it on the news this morning!"

"Oh my God! Who?" I asked.

"Cindy [a registered nurse] and Jennifer [a nursing assistant] from the nursing home. They were on their way to Eau Claire after the p.m. shift. Cindy was driving when the car slipped on snow and ice and ended up sideways at the top of a ridge entering the other lane. Dave Brown [also an RN in the nursing home and a husband to one of my RNs in the hospital] hit them broadside coming from the other direction, and both girls were killed on impact. Dave was injured, but he's okay. Obviously he's in bad shape, since he feels responsible for killing Cindy and Jennifer, even though it wasn't his fault."

My mind instantly called to the forefront Cindy's image. She was a tall, strawberry blonde girl around the age of thirty. Her hair was bobbed, and freckles peppered the bridge of her nose, making her appear pixie-like. She was very thin with translucent skin and an infectious smile and laugh. The residents in the nursing home loved her. I tried to envision the other employee, since I didn't know all the nursing home staff members individually.

"Was Jennifer the young pregnant girl?" I asked.

"Yes, and she just got married two weeks ago," Becky said with grave sadness in her voice. "There's something else," Becky said cautiously.

"What more can there be?" I said, a bit of shock and denial grabbing hold.

"Inside Cindy's purse in the car, the officers found a pile of medications from the nursing home."

"I'll get showered, dressed, and be right there," I said, cutting her off abruptly.

None of the staff knew that we had called in a Drug Enforcement Agency representative recently to investigate the loss of medications from the nursing home. We had suspicions Cindy might be involved, but the investigation was being launched just as she was killed. I guess we had our proof right there in the mangled wreckage. They found residents' bottles of pills in her purse; alongside unit dose packaging of medications she had charted out as being given to the residents, but which found their way to her handbag instead.

Nelly

I was sick to my stomach. In the days to come, the shock wore off, and sadness enveloped the entire building of residents, patients, physicians, and staff. As small communities often do, they grieved as one. We held a remembrance service at the hospital and nursing home facility. I had to lead the service and eulogize each of the deceased. I could barely choke out words, thinking about Jennifer lying in the brown casket dressed in her wedding gown, a small, lifeless bump protruding under her stilled hands.

Her husband, now a widower, looked at me from the front seat, eyes imploring me to shed some light on understanding this tragedy. He was a tall, gangly young man barely able to grow a mustache, a shadowy hairline visible above his lip. In the flip of a switch, his life went from a honeymooning groom and expectant dad … to nothing. Dark bags of skin hung under his eyes as his brown gaze sought mine for solace in words I could only transmit by rote.

My family taught me that when in emotional pain, drink alcohol. Numb the pain at all costs. My years working on the oncology unit reinforced this valuable lesson. I had seen a fair amount of death and tragedy in my short life, but none that affected me as much as these two young people. At that moment, I was desperate for emotional release. Drinking obviously was out of the question at work, so Glinda, being as clever as she was, beckoned me down a new avenue.

During a break in the memorial service, I slithered away down the carpeted hall as if retreating toward my office. Taking a sharp left behind the unattended nursing station, I entered the pharmacy storage room that staff nurses used to store and dispense patient medications.

A black garbage bag called to me from the dark, sterile corner. The half-filled bag stored outdated medications that I had recently gathered to return to pharmaceutical companies for disposal and hospital credit. Being a small community hospital, accurate record keeping wasn't done regarding medications, so no inventory held me at bay.

I reached into the now-open bag and dug around until I found what I was looking for. As devastated as I was feeling, I was hopeful

113

the black bag would swallow me whole so that I wouldn't have to face those families' grief again. No such luck. Retrieving what I needed, I reached for a large manila envelope on the counter and stuffed sheets of orange, oval pill packets inside. With the pills successfully stuffed in the concealed sleeve, I hastened toward my office to stash my cache of pain pills in my briefcase. Eli Lilly and Co. would never miss the extra hundred absconded Darvocet, and Lord knew I certainly could put them to good use.

In my office bathroom, I released a couple of pills from their foiled beds. I took a cold drink of water to wash them down and leaned precariously over the sink, hands resting on each side of the porcelain bowl to steady my stance. My heart knew I had crossed another dangerous line, and my disappointment in myself weighed heavily on my soul. Within a minute or two, I began to feel the familiar chemical relief embrace me.

I looked in the mirror and didn't recognize the person before me. The woman staring back at me from the mirror was a drunk, fraud, and now thief. I looked for any sign of recognition of the human being I used to be, but all I saw looking back at me were expressionless, almost lifeless, green eyes. With new medicinal fortification, I was able to get the renewal of energy I desperately needed before returning to the mourners gathered down the hall.

The irony of the situation never crossed my ill mind. Here I was leading a memorial service for two young lives taken. The driver was being investigated for drug theft and was clearly a suspected addict with a serious problem. Who knows if Cindy was under the influence while driving that winter night? I never did find out, although my suspicions were that she had been significantly impaired. And what do I choose to do on the heels of such tragedy? Follow in Cindy's footsteps. Only in my mind I wasn't stealing medications, because these pain pills were being returned as outdated. They were going to be destroyed anyway. No big deal. No harm done. Right?

That night, I went home and typed my resignation. After a sleepless night, I submitted it to the administrator the next morning. After I tendered my resignation, I called Michael and told him I had quit.

"Are you crazy? Michael yelled, in a tirade. "What are we going to do about money, paying bills, and health insurance, for God's sake?"

"I am miserable," I said in a barely audible, meek voice. "You have no idea what I just went through. What about me?"

I guess that didn't count. He hung up on me.

Several months later, I received a part-time job offer four hours away at a large hospital in Green Bay. I told Michael I was going to take this part-time quality job, and if he wanted to join me, he was welcome. I needed to be closer to home. He decided to join me. We were packing up our lives and everything familiar to leave Eau Claire for a part-time job on the other side of the state.

A couple of days before we were set to leave, Michael was lounging in the bathtub in the house we were renting. The shrilly landline rang out, alerting our Golden Retriever to join in the reverberation.

"Is Michael there?" a refined male voice asked.

"Sure, just a minute please," I answered.

Living in the cordless telephone era, I walked to the bathroom, my hand covering the microphone end of the phone. Pushing open the door, I saw Michael ensconced in bubbles and lather, looking like a little boy settled in for his nightly bath. All he needed was a rubber ducky, and the picture would be complete.

"Someone for you. I don't know who it is," I said rather hurriedly, intent to get back to packing up our kitchenware.

As I shut the bathroom door leaving him to his phone call, I got the impression by his greeting that it might be a call he had been expecting. I heard his enthusiastic murmurs through the door, shrugged to myself, and went back to the task at hand.

A half hour later, Michael came out of the bathroom wrapped in a fluffy white towel and smelling sweet and clean. A warm essence left over from the heat of the bath water on Michael's skin floated past me as he quickly advanced toward the refrigerator. He pulled out a huge bottle of red wine.

"What's the occasion?" I asked, a little resentful that I was doing all the preparatory work for the move while he got to relax and lounge at will.

"I was just offered a job as the manager of investment banking at a bank in Green Bay." A broad grin encompassed his handsome face as he grabbed unpacked, large orbed glasses to house the wine.

"What?" I said. "Why didn't you tell me? I didn't think you were still in the running for that job?"

"Well, I just got offered the job and start next week," Michael said, relief filling his utterance.

"I'm so happy for you ... for us ... what perfect timing," I enthused, matching his level of excitement and relief.

We drank, celebrated, and made love that night, feeling like a couple of kids on the brink of a new adventure, a new city, and new jobs. Life was looking up indeed!

Michael and I began drinking alcohol almost daily. What started out in the beginning as drinking on weekends while going out on dates developed into coming home from work and relaxing with a glass of wine or beer before dinner. Then I began to drink after dinner too. I think being a woman and a lighter weight, the alcohol affected me more than Michael. I felt as if I were struggling to stay ahead of the game.

I would buy cheap wine boxes and place them in the closet. Having the boxes came in handy, because no one could tell how much I was drinking. When emptied, I would replace one box with another, identical one. Then I would quickly hide the old box and bury it in the garbage cans. The frequency of replacing the boxes was speeding up, so I'd buy a box at one store, and the next time buy one at another store. That way if the same clerk worked each time, they wouldn't know what a lush I was turning into.

It was about this time that I happened upon bottles of alcohol hidden in the basement where Michael kept his workroom for doing various woodworking projects. I would go into the garage looking for a hammer or other tool for a routine household fix and stumble across a half-filled bottle of blackberry brandy housed in a brown paper bag. Of course, who was I to say anything, since I was hiding my wine consumption? Only I was hiding my drinking in plain sight. Somehow that made me superior in my mind.

Both of us, despite our alcohol consumption, were doing well at work and maintaining some balance. There were many times consequences to my drinking behavior could have been problematic, but thus far I had been able to preserve daily life without experiencing DUIs, legal troubles, or relationship or job losses. One episode that comes to mind happened prior to my getting a job.

I had to take a pre-employment physical that included blood work. I was concerned about the lab work portion; because I knew people with chronic excess alcohol consumption could have elevated liver enzymes.

Sitting in the nurses' office getting my lab work done, I said a quick prayer to my grandma and asked her to get me through this physical, as our livelihood depended upon me getting this job. There was another nurse getting her lab work drawn at the same time as me, and her name was Robin. We struck up a conversation and found out we were scheduled to be in orientation together once we got through this pre-employment step of the process.

A week later, my future boss called me and said, "Welcome aboard. I just got word you are cleared to work."

"I passed my physical?" I said, somewhat surprised.

"Yes. Did you expect a problem?" my boss asked questioningly.

"No, not at all. I'm just anxious to start work," I said quickly, dismissing my initial surprise.

"Oh, well ... then we look forward to seeing you on Monday."

"Thanks, I'm looking forward to it too," I said with all sincerity.

Feeling a great sense of liberation after that phone call, I got busy preparing for work on Monday, once again lending credence in my own mind to the thought that maybe my drinking wasn't as bad as I thought.

During orientation the following week, I sat next to Robin.

"The funniest thing happened to me after seeing you last time," she leaned over and said.

"What?" I asked, somewhat disinterested in her chatter.

"Remember that day we had our blood drawn? My blood work showed elevated liver enzymes, and I don't even drink alcohol! I had to go back and have it re-drawn three days later, and they were fine then. Isn't that weird? I wonder if the lab made a mistake or something."

"That's crazy!" I lowered my eyes to the mountain of employment paperwork in front of me. I could feel my face flush as my anxiety level and general paranoia heightened. My synapses were trying quickly to figure out how the switch in blood work was made. I realized lab personnel must have put her name label on my blood work, and vice versa.

"I wonder why that happened," I said, gaining composure. "Maybe the testing equipment in the lab is off." I knew full well that it was my prayers being answered by Grandma. I looked skyward and said a silent "thank you." Deep down, I knew my dishonest life would eventually be exposed, but so far, so good!

After a couple of years working at the bank, Michael had the financial business department growing. The investment section of the bank was exceeding all sales goals, and he was certainly growing as a young professional. He was mastering speaking engagements, and surpassing everyone else in their production.

He came home one day looking pale and shaky.

"What's wrong?" I asked.

"I got fired today," Michael said.

"What?" I said in utter disbelief.

nelly

Michael sat with resignation in the rocker recliner in the living room of the house we had just purchased. Although Michael was a practical joker by nature, I knew this time he was serious.

"Oh my God. What happened?" I asked. "You were hitting your sales numbers out of the park!"

"Yeah, but there were a couple of women there that can't stand me, and in the end, they won out."

"What are we going to do now? We have this house to pay for." Since I was the person paying the bills, I started to panic, knowing full well what would happen with our income cut in half.

"Start looking for another job, I guess," Michael said somewhat flippantly, yet defeated.

Michael spent five months working on the house. He was so embarrassed about being "let go" that he spent most of his time holed up in the house, feigning "project work." It was almost as if he was paralyzed. I would come home every day to a man sinking lower into depression and increasing his drinking with each resume sent and rejected. He was entertaining any and all job opportunities, since the economy was still stagnant. One such job posting he applied to be selling fire extinguishers door to door. He was becoming quite desperate to work again.

Six months into the job loss, he came home with several lobsters and wine. Living on a shoestring budget, I immediately flew into a verbal strike. Michael ignored my ranting and set the table very patiently. He lit candles as he let me bellow on. I softened as he continued to putter around the kitchen. He was saying little. Often he would let me wear myself out with my verbal diatribes.

As we sat down to eat the succulent lobster meat, he poured me a glass of wine and clinked glasses, saying "Here's to my new job! You'll never guess where I got a new position."

At that point I didn't care if he was employed washing dishes. My only concern was keeping a roof over our heads and bill collectors at bay.

"Where?" I said.

"Aid Association for Lutherans (AAL) in Appleton," he replied.

We both started roaring hysterically. "You have got to be kidding me?" I said as I doubled over in convulsed laughter.

A couple of days later, the phone rang.

"Why the hell didn't you tell me Michael got a job at AAL," Susie demanded.

"What do you mean?" I answered playfully.

"I was in a meeting today, and Caroline mentioned she had just hired a Michael Branson. Imagine how stupid I felt when I realized she'd hired my brother-in-law, and I didn't know anything about it!"

"Well, Michael has been out of work awhile, so we were celebrating privately before we told you, but we were getting around to it," I said, starting to get annoyed at Susie's continued displeasure.

That evening, I told Michael about my conversation with my sister.

"Well," he said, "it isn't like she did anything to help me get a job. She could have recommended me to someone there, since she knew they were starting up the financial branch of the business. But no, I had to drive past the building and on a fluke go in and apply. I was asked to write a one-page business letter, then met with Caroline and got hired on the spot. Susie and John have never liked me, so screw them!"

Susie took Michael's hiring as a personal affront for some reason. She had been working at AAL for about seven years and was quite accomplished. She had been a math teacher at a local high school before getting the job at AAL. She was the head of underwriting for insurance products, and I guess she felt it was "her" company. How dare we not tell her Michael was now an employee!

After Michael began work, my sister would be in line in the cafeteria waiting to get lunch, and Michael would be stationed a couple of people in back of her. She wouldn't even acknowledge his existence. I thought she was still upset about us not telling her that Michael got a job there, but her behavior toward him never changed in the many years he worked there. As he climbed in status at the company, her bristled nature toward him continued to escalate.

Paradoxically, we would have family gatherings for various occasions, and after Susie had ingested a few cocktails, Michael magically became her best friend—to the exclusion of the rest of the family. John, her husband, would start fuming because Susie and Michael became close confidantes, talking about the company and various employees. They would scrutinize someone they knew, and their ongoing conversation left the rest of us feeling like outsiders. After visiting my family, Michael would comment about how different Susie treated him at their home compared to work.

"That's because she has a few drinks in her and loosens up a bit," I explained.

After a family gathering, Monday morning it would be business as usual. Susie wouldn't acknowledge Michael at work. He thought it was the strangest thing, but blew it off as Susie just acting quirky. We thought she may be jealous as Michael's career path began a steady incline toward the top, surpassing the role Susie held in the company.

Michael was sought after for speaking engagements, he won marketing awards, was voted number one wholesaler, and received various other professional recognitions for his work. He started at the bottom answering phones in the customer service center at this company and worked up to the Vice President of Sales and Marketing. I was very proud of his accomplishments. My career was on an even keel at the hospital, and we were in a comfort zone. Never comfortable with a status quo existence, I single-handedly decided now was the right time to have a baby!

CHAPTER 23

BABY

It was nearing Christmas, 1993, in Green Bay, WI. Michael had bought a motorcycle the previous summer and needed a leather bomber jacket. I bought him a soft, brown leather jacket he had been eyeing for some time. I knew he would love it. I felt it was going to be a special Christmas this year.

Wednesday, December 22, I was at work sitting at my desk, but I couldn't concentrate on what I had been doing. Anxiety level rising, I just needed to get home. Luckily, another gift I bought Michael was arriving that day, and I needed to be home for the delivery.

Running out of the hospital, I entered the four-story parking ramp, found my red truck, hopped in, and drove a few miles down Webster Avenue toward Bittersweet Avenue in Alloeuz. I easily slipped the truck into our garage and shut the door quickly for fear "Gladys Kravitz," our neighbor, would espy my vehicle. If she saw me, there would be an inquiry on our nightly walk, and I didn't want to deal with her suspicions.

I was in the bathroom reading directions carefully as if my life depended on it. I peed on the pregnancy kit stick, following instructions precisely. As I was finishing up, the doorbell rang. The furniture truck had pulled into our driveway, and two men were standing at the door hanging on to Michael's new rocker recliner.

They entered the house and navigated around a very excited, 110-pound, tail-swishing Golden Retriever. She loved anyone coming to the door, except the mail lady. The men placed the new furniture piece in our cozy living room where I had carved out a spot. Atty immediately jumped on the chair, christening its arrival.

I was keeping track of my watch carefully to make sure I was timing things without so much as a misstep. I thanked the men and hastened them through the entryway, bolting the front door tightly. I didn't want anyone intruding on my special moment. Fear and excitement gripped my chest so tightly I could hardly breathe. I was thirty-three years old. My whole life flashed before me, and I felt this was the moment I had been waiting for my entire life. I said a silent prayer and asked God and Grandma's help in delivering a special gift.

I almost fainted crossing the threshold to the bathroom. I felt like I was finishing a marathon, and the goal was within arm's reach. Everything happened in slow motion as I reached for the pencil-thin, white stick that held my hopes and dreams in its small glass window. I shakily picked up the stick, gripping each end as if it were weighty. My eyes were clenched shut.

Taking a deep breath, I didn't want to open my eyes for fear I would be utterly disappointed. As I opened my eyes ever so slightly, I saw a blurry red "plus" symbol in the tiny glass window. The next thing I knew, I was sitting in the new rocker recliner, clutching the little white stick, tears of joy streaming down my face.

I remember sitting in the minister's tiny office during pre-marital counseling when he asked us about wanting kids. Michael said "yes" with little emotion, adding that "a couple of kids would be nice one day." Although we really never talked much about kids thereafter, his stance was, "If it happens, it happens; if it doesn't, it doesn't." Michael was more into his career and definitely more focused on material things than emotions of the heart.

It was my belief that early in life Michael learned to put walls around his emotions for protection, and subsequently there wasn't much depth to his "feeling" side. He was a "loner from little on" his mother told me. For me, it seemed like keeping things on a superficial level protected his inner core. Having children would demand a crack in the armor of emotions that I think he was unwilling to face, so having children was a subject we tended to avoid.

When I came to the conclusion that I wasn't getting younger and the time was right to start trying, I began like I did everything in life— get a plan and go step by step. Step one was to limit my drinking and get into better shape on a physical level. So instead of coming home from work and hitting the wine box, I went down into the basement and worked out on a stair climber for up to sixty minutes. Then I would prepare something for dinner and go for a walk with my neighbor. The exercise did for Glinda what alcohol had done—it provided a high of sorts, only the high was from endorphins and not ethanol.

After I was on a healthier track physically, I needed to pay close attention to my monthly cycle. I tracked my period for about six months while I was getting in shape. I decided to go to the drugstore and buy an ovulation kit to predict my most fertile days.

In early November 1993, we attended our neighbor's son's wedding. Per our usual behavior, both Michael and I had a good time and had too much to drink. After getting home at one in the morning, I was ready for action, knowing full well timing was optimal for reproduction. Unknowingly, Michael complied with my plan. The next morning, I don't even think Michael remembered the activities of the night before. We were both hung over and licking our wounds.

Tears subsiding and reality setting in, I now had to figure out a way to tell Michael. I was fearful of his reaction, because I wanted him to feel what I was feeling in that moment—a bursting, joyful heart. If he reacted negatively, as he usually did to matters that were important to me, I would be absolutely crushed.

Two days later on Christmas Eve, we decided to exchange gifts. I was as nervous as I could be. It was show time. We exchanged the usual gifts, and then I gave him one last package. It was a beautifully wrapped box with red and silver glistening paper. I had made a home-made bow of silken ribbon, and I thought it was the most beautiful package I had ever created.

"Wow, this is beautiful. You outdid yourself … thanks!"

"Well, open it, silly. I hope you like it," I tittered nervously.

Michael was like a child with a present. Ignoring the beautiful wrapping, he ripped into the gift, anxious to see what the package held. He opened the box and saw his coveted leather coat.

"Wow, you got exactly the one I wanted," Michael exclaimed.

"I hope you like it. Try it on and see if it fits," I said with a hesitant voice, my heart about to beat out of my chest.

Michael stood and put on the coat, hands running down the soft leather front.

"It's beautiful and fits great!" Michael said, face beaming. He bent over to where I was sitting on the carpeted floor, giving me a whisper of kiss on my lips. "Thank you so much. I love it!" He zipped up the front and continued to prance around the living room, preening like a peacock. As he modeled the coat, his hands slipped inside the pockets, and a look of puzzlement spread across his face. He pulled out a small square gift. "What is this?" Michael said, looking quizzically.

"Open it up!" I said, eyes brimming with tears.

Michael opened the box and pulled out a pair of small, white knit baby booties with blue ribbon weaved around the ankles. At first, total confusion flashed across his face. Then again as if everything was in slow motion, he looked at me questioningly. Tears fell into my lap as I shook my head up and down, indicating "yes."

Michael fell to his knees and embraced me. "I can't believe it," he said.

I asked him if he was happy.

"More in a state of shock," he said. "Someone left baby booties in the pocket by mistake. I'll have to return this coat to its owner," he said mockingly.

I playfully hit him in the arm as he asked me if I was feeling okay.

"Great, never better," I said.

He sat silently in the recliner, rocking back and forth and holding the baby booties with his coat on, eyes closed, and taking in the enormity of the moment.

Within the first two months of my pregnancy, I had the baby room painted a soft blue and had bought a choo choo train stencil that took weeks to apply in about twenty different steps. The train moved along tracks bordering the room. At the half-way point, smoke bellowed up the wall. I knew I was pregnant with a boy, and although I hadn't discussed it with Michael, my name for him was William, after my grandfather who had died atop the train long ago.

Week ten, I went to my OB appointment and was excited to hear the heartbeat. The doctor applied the cold, clear jelly to my abdomen, making small talk along the way. To her, it was business as usual, but to me, it was a monumental moment. The ultrasound machine was hooked up to the flattened pad covering my soft belly. As the doctor ran her hand over the jelled pad, moving it side to side and up and down, staring at the fuzzy ultrasound screen, the excitement I felt soon faded as a look of puzzlement and concern fleeted across the doctor's face.

"What's wrong?" I asked, panic beginning to swell.

"Nothing yet, I'm just not hearing a heartbeat. I need to run some labs to test your hormone levels and make sure we're on track. It may be that it's just too early to hear it," the doctor said in a pretty upbeat fashion, although I could sense underlying concern.

Weeks of intermittent hCG (Human Chorionic Gonadotropin) hormone tests revealed my hormone level decreasing instead of increasing like expected in a normal pregnancy. I was distraught, and Michael was distant and mute.

I was still in the midst of monitoring my hormone levels, hoping to see improvement, when I went out to retrieve the daily mail. Inside was a small stuffed teddy bear from Enfamil, a company that makes baby formula. Through the doctor's office, the company is notified about impending births and sends the prospective parents a small gift; hoping parents will purchase their formula.

Entering the house, I started feeling some cramps and went to the bathroom. As I was sitting on the toilet, blood and blood clots started to pour out of me. Clutching the teddy bear, I screamed, "No, you can't have him!" as the red river continued to flow. I had never seen so much blood in my life. I stuffed as many pads as I could get in my bottom and stumbled to the phone to call Michael. He was at least a half hour away at work, and he said he would come home.

"I don't have a half hour. I need to get to the doctor now," I said, panicked.

Beginning to feel faint, I had a surge of adrenalin and ended up driving myself down to the doctor's office, which luckily were only minutes away. She put me on the exam table as she screamed at a nearby aid for a bucket to catch the blood that continued to gush out of me. She said they needed to wheel me across the street to the hospital where I worked and get me to surgery for an emergency D & C (a procedure in which they can scrape the lining of the uterus). I pretty much blacked out at that point. I woke up in the post-recovery room with a childless womb and a broken heart.

Resting in bed that night, emotionally and physically exhausted from the happenings of the day, I got up to go to the bathroom, and the bleeding started once again. I told Michael that something wasn't right and I had to get to the hospital before I bled to death.

"Okay," Michael said, turning over and going back to sleep.

I drove myself back to the hospital and to the emergency room. There, the ER doctor told me my uterus wasn't contracting after the surgery, so he manually had to cause the uterus to clamp down on itself, whatever that meant. I swear, I looked down and the man had his arm up to his elbow inside my body. I was so numb at that point I didn't care if he crawled up inside me to stop the bleeding or get my uterus to do flips if that's what he wanted. Whatever he did, worked, and I drove back to the house in time for Michael to get up for work. I told him what I had been through, and as he left the house he said, "Well, I'm glad they got the bleeding to stop."

I sat in the recliner the entire day, clutching the teddy bear. I looked down at the small creature, and it looked like it too was shedding tears as my fallen droplets lay unabsorbed on his brown, furry face. Atty was lying at my feet, and she looked up at me with her saddened brown eyes as if she could feel my pain.

Michael promised that he would do anything he could so we could try again once I had recovered and the doctor said it was safe to try to get pregnant again. His willingness to try for another pregnancy carried me through, and I recovered physically and emotionally relatively quickly. As long as Michael was willing to try, I figured I would get pregnant right away. After all, the first pregnancy happened without effort at all.

So began the odyssey of trying to get pregnant. True to his word, Michael was a trooper. I would monitor my monthly cycle, and we would try to conceive when the ovulation predictor kit told us the time was optimal. After months of getting my hopes up only to be dashed by a trip to the bathroom, I was becoming desperate. The doctor put me on Clomid, which in infertile women can stimulate ovaries to produce eggs in an effort to increase the likelihood of conception.

As part of the monthly doctor visit to see how the Clomid was working on my ovaries, the doctor stuck a vaginal wand in me to see how my ovaries were responding to the medication. A picture would develop on the ultrasound screen, and I was getting pretty good at reading the fuzzy black and white static. The ovary actually looked like a piece of Swiss cheese, the round holes were where the ovary would pop out an egg. The process became very clinical and scientific, which for me wasn't a problem, since I was a nurse and interested in every aspect of the process.

The problem came with Michael. At one point after I was ruled out as the source of infertility, the doctor suggested getting Michael tested. Although Michael was willing to go along with the intercourse part of reproduction, going through the steps of getting himself tested was not something he was interested in doing.

The doctor knew how much having a child meant to me. "Well, if he won't get tested, we could test him through you," she suggested.

"What do you mean?" I asked, confused.

"Well, next month when you come in to check your ovaries and you have intercourse on the specified day, you come in and we'll take the semen sample from you and test it."

"I didn't know you could do that?"

"Usually men will cooperate with testing, but it doesn't sound like Michael wants to assist with the testing, so we'll work around him."

"Oh, okay," I said, relieved that there was a next step in the process. I was used to working around Michael, anyway. So that is what we did. We discovered that Michael had a minor infection of some sort, so he was put on antibiotics, which cleared the infection, and we continued along in the process. In the beginning, I was hopeful; as time went on ... less so.

Three years after my miscarriage and all the ups and downs of fertility treatment, we had both given up and decided it wasn't "meant to be." It got to the point where I was an emotional wreck each disappointing month, and Michael really didn't know how to make it better. Getting pregnant had been my only focus for three years. I can't imagine as a man being required to "perform" on demand, and the clinical nature of reproduction became a strain on both of us and hard on our relationship.

I quit my job, we put our house up for sale, and it sold the first weekend. We decided to move closer to where Michael was working, and I accepted a new position with a Health Maintenance Organization (HMO). A fresh start was what we needed.

During my last visit to the doctor, I told her we were done. No more probes, meds, and ovary pictures or testing. It was time to move on. The doctor thought that was a fair decision, but decided to look at my ovaries one more time. She said they looked "really good" this month if we decided to try one more time. I told Michael the results, we gave it one more try, and, miraculously, it worked.

I felt different almost immediately, with breast tenderness, nausea, and other symptoms, but I didn't tell Michael, as we had been through so many ups and downs during this process. I wanted to tell him, but didn't know how to this time. So I just reveled in my own little secret, daring to hope things would work out this time.

One weekend we were cleaning out our basement, deciding what to toss or keep as we prepared for the move to the new house. Digging through cupboards where various non-essential items had been tossed over the years, I ran across a book that had been given to Michael by someone as a joke during our first pregnancy. It was Bill Cosby's book, *Fatherhood*. I looked at the smiling, kind face of Bill Cosby and thought it was an omen. Now was the perfect moment.

I walked to Michael and handed him Bill's smiling portrait and said, "You may want to pack this one."

Michael looked at it. "I think we can toss that," he said, irritated by my interruption of his packing.

"YOU ... MAY ... WANT ... TO ... PACK ... THIS ... ONE," I said, emphasizing each word loudly.

He stopped what he was doing and paid attention, probably thinking I had lost my mind in the heat, dust, and dirt of the basement.

"Okay, if that's what you want," he said, shrugging and trying to accommodate a crazy wife's wishes.

All I could do was start laughing uncontrollably. Michael looked at me like I had really lost my mind for good this time, so I sat down on the couch. When I started regaining composure, I said, "I'm trying to tell you I'm pregnant, goofball. We are finally going to have a baby!"

We were both utterly emotionally exhausted from the previous three years of monthly ups and downs, buying and selling a house, packing up everything we owned, and embarking on a new job, journey, and city. The news we had been anticipating for a long time had finally come, and all we could do was look at each other amongst the grit, grime, and pile of boxes. Wordless and feeling numb, neither of us had any emotional reserves left, so we sat there on the couch, not daring to mutter a sound.

CHAPTER 24

1997

I loved being pregnant and felt great. It was the first time in my life I didn't care about what I ate, how much weight I gained, or really anything at all. I just enjoyed living in the moment and growing a new life inside me. It was truly a miracle getting to this point, and another making it through each trimester. I had a real feeling of peace, perhaps for the first and only time in my life. Glinda was at bay. I didn't engage in any behavior that would threaten the pregnancy or the daughter I was carrying. It was the first time I felt my life had purpose; therefore, I wasn't self-destructive.

It was a bitterly cold sunny day. Sunday, February 23, 1997. Being an early riser, Michael was out killing time on Lake Winnebago, driving around in my truck on the shallow lake's ice. I got up about 8:00 a.m. and wobbled to the bathroom. I was due to deliver a baby girl in one week, March 2, which happened to be Georgia's birthday. After gaining a total of sixty-five pounds, I was ready any time now. I was tired of using my belly as a shelf to eat off and having feet the size of an elephant. My bags had been packed for weeks, and like everything in my life, a list of chores to get ready prior to delivery was complete.

Nelly

Instead of water breaking, which could signal the start of labor, my water decided to start leaking slowly early that Sunday morning. I called Michael and told him to get ready, because our baby girl might be ready to enter the world that day.

I called the hospital, letting them know about my physical changes.

"No hurry," they said. "Take your time. It doesn't sound like she's in too big a hurry to enter the world."

I decided we'd leave for the hospital at 3:30 p.m. Being a nurse; I wanted to arrive after change of shift. I wanted to wait until the nurse assigned to me was beginning her 3–11 shift, so she could be with me the entire time throughout the labor and delivery process. I was pretty stoic on the drive to the hospital. Michael and I were making small talk. I do remember him asking me if it was difficult not drinking alcohol for nine months. I said "not at all," and I was being honest. It wasn't hard to abstain from alcohol with a life growing inside of me.

Michael was drinking on a daily basis at that point, and I continued to find bottles hidden in the garage or throughout the house. Maybe he was thinking now would be a good time to quit drinking too. I don't know the impetus for the question, but I needed to be focused on myself and the baby, so I let it pass without giving it much further thought.

After getting settled in the hospital bed, all the cords and appropriate apparatus for monitoring blood pressure, oxygen saturation levels, and contractions were attached. I told the nurse that I was continuing to leak amniotic fluid.

"Well, let's just check you out then," she said cheerily.

After donning gloves, the nurse did a vaginal check on me. With a wrinkled brow, she said, "Huh, I think I'll get another nurse on shift to check you out too. I felt something pointy!"

Another nurse entered the room, snapped on latex gloves, and repeated the exam.

"Well, that is interesting," she said in a questioning fashion. "I think I just stuck my finger in her mouth. If she's coming down face first, that's not a good presentation, so I'm going to call Dr. Bartly."

Fifteen minutes later, Dr. Bartly swaggered into my room, sucking on a lollipop. He was a handsome man with grey and black speckled hair, and about sixty years of age. After some introductory chit chat about how glad he was that we called him because he was in the middle of doing his taxes and would much rather be here, he got down to business and gloved up as well.

After a quick exam, he turned around, took a scrub set from a nearby table, and threw the pair across the room at Michael sitting in the chair. Michael had bought a new video camera for the big event and was engrossed in trying to figure how to operate the new gadget, pretty much oblivious to the attention being paid to me. The scrubs landed on top of the video camera and caught Michael off guard.

"You better change clothes. We're going to do a C-section and will take Nelly into the operating room shortly," Dr. Bartly said nonchalantly.

"Oh no, I'm not going in to any operating room!" Michael stated defiantly.

"Oh yes you are. This is your baby too," I said, giving Michael marching orders.

Within two hours of walking through the hospital doors, our daughter, Janelle, was born. A healthy seven and a half pound, twenty-inch-long baby girl with a set of lungs on her that didn't quit! We reveled in the moment like every new parent who learns that their child is healthy, has ten fingers and toes, and all the proper parts. After three days, I was discharged and all hell broke loose.

My mind had been so focused on getting pregnant and having a healthy pregnancy and delivery that I hadn't given much thought to life after baby. At age thirty-seven, I had to realize that I was indeed a new mom with an infant 100 percent dependent on me. Although

Michael had given great press to how he would help out when the baby came, reality didn't play out that way.

Georgia came down to stay and help out intermittently over the next several months, and I couldn't have made it without her assistance. In the beginning, she would take the night shift and I would do the day shift. Janelle was up every hour to two hours at the beginning of her life, and had a set of lungs on her that she was not afraid to use. The doctor called her colicky. Michael nicknamed her the "rat," and although it didn't sound like a nice name, he meant it in a loving way. Due to the large head she inherited from her dad's side, he also nicknamed her Yoda, "melon-head," and all kinds of other terms of endearment. Mostly, "the rat" stuck. I would look at Janelle and repeat a common line in those early days: "I love you, but don't like you very much!" My life changed 180 degrees, and Michael's didn't change one bit. He went on his merry way, pretty much oblivious to the rigors of new parenthood. I became resentful … just a bit!

My anxiety level was at an all-time high. I broke out in hives I was so stressed. I was operating on minimal, if any, sleep. Michael was traveling for his job. He was now a wholesaler, which required traveling throughout the United States, speaking, and motivating sales forces. When home, he virtually crashed to rest for the next round of travel.

I was alone with an infant who took 100 percent of my time and effort, and I was falling fast. Depression set in. The doctors diagnosed me with post-partum depression. I started taking an antidepressant. I would cry all day long. Michael looked at me like I was crazy. Of course, I really was.

"You have everything you always wanted," he'd say. "Pull yourself up by the bootstraps now and snap out of it!" He didn't understand the chemical and hormonal imbalance in my body, and I wasn't helping myself much.

I began drinking daily, and if necessary, I'd begin mid-morning. I was managing to take care of Janelle's needs, but not mine. I would begin the day by opening a can of Diet Pepsi, and after about half the contents were gone; I'd add some whiskey, or whatever other alcohol was in the house, to the can. That way, no one would know I was drinking. If I did laundry, I might have a bottle of wine stored up above in the laundry cabinets. I did lots of laundry in those early days. Didn't everyone have a bottle close by to make it through daily chores?

After about three months, I needed to return to work, initially working ten hour days. This really threw me into a tizzy. At times I was so disoriented, I'd get up at 11:00 p.m., get ready for work, and Michael would have to point out that it was the middle of the night, not the morning. In the morning fog, I would wake up digging through the bed linens, searching for Janelle, thinking she was in bed with us and fearful I had rolled over on her and smothered her. As I was struggling, Michael was excelling in his job. I was sinking; he was swimming.

Had it not been for Georgia, I wouldn't have made it through that initial period of time. She knew I was depressed, and she was suspicious about my drinking I am sure, but she didn't say anything to me. She focused on taking care of her only granddaughter and helping me out. She would bake cookies, make homemade meals, do our laundry, and watch Janelle so I could get my hair done, take an hour to shop, or do whatever I needed to do. Half-jokingly, I would say, "Mom, would you marry me?" She was the sole support and assistance I had, and I loved and was indebted to her. If I hadn't had her there, I would have surely ended up hospitalized in the loony bin.

As Janelle got out of the newborn stage, Glinda leveled out a bit, and I was able to maintain some semblance of a routine to my new life.

Michael flew home from New York one Monday. The next day, Tuesday, July 14, he was getting ready for work and said, "I don't feel so hot!"

"What's wrong?" I said dismissively.

"I've got a sore stomach," he said, grimacing slightly as he touched his lower left abdomen gently with his fingertips.

"Well, usually appendicitis is more on the right, so you should be okay." I was still in the dismissive stage, busying myself with filling baby bottles with formula before heading out for work myself. So off to work we went.

When I got home that evening, Michael was in bed resting. He had gone to the doctor that day, which for him was highly unusual. If he wasn't dying, he didn't seek medical attention. I started to pay closer attention to what he was telling me.

"What did the doctor say?" I asked as I gingerly sat on the edge of the bed. Michael was looking a bit pale. Automatically feeling his forehead, like a mother would with a child, I noticed that he felt warm to my touch.

"They took an X-ray and said my colon was full of gas, and I might be FOS ... full of shit, in laymen terms. They recommended trying an enema."

Being the ever-ready nurse, I gave him an enema and he disappeared into the bathroom for quite a long time ... maybe an hour.

"Any results," I asked clinically.

"No, none," Michael answered in a concerned tone.

"Do you have any pain, passing gas, anything?" I asked, mentally checking off the questions that came naturally. Having a stethoscope handy, I listened to his abdomen and heard active bowel sounds in all four abdominal quadrants, so I knew that was a good sign.

As the next few hours progressed, Michael became more lethargic. His temperature started to climb, and he began looking more ashen in color. All he wanted to do was sleep. I tried persuading him to let me take him to urgent care or the emergency room of the hospital, but he simply mumbled, half in and out of consciousness, "I'll be fine in the morning."

At 9:00 p.m., Michael's temperature topped at 105 degrees.

"I'm taking you to the emergency room," I said. "I have Janelle ready to go. Michael, this could be something serious!"

Michael was barely able to rouse. Moving as slowly as a sloth would, he pulled on some nearby sweats. He didn't have the energy to protest anymore, so we took off for the hospital.

Five months after our daughter was born, we entered the same hospital with Michael hobbling into the emergency department. A young, slender, female doctor with dark hair pulled back in a pony took Michael's history, did a thorough physical exam, and ordered the appropriate X-rays and blood tests. By this time, Michael was experiencing increased abdominal pain, so morphine was administered quickly once an IV was established.

Waiting for hours in the ER department is the usual routine, and this visit was no exception. I only had a doctor's swivel chair to sit on for hours. Janelle, in her infant seat, was sleeping on the floor next to me. I was subconsciously rocking Janelle's infant carrier with my left leg, trying to keep her subdued while maintaining my own balance. I gazed at the beautiful infant sleeping so angelically in her car seat, not having a clue about anything going on around her. I then looked at Michael lying on the ER bed, looking grey, and my mind began to go places I didn't want to think about. What if this child grows up without a father? I'd be on my own raising a child while barely able to manage my own life. I had worked myself up into a state of worry just as the young doctor strolled into the room.

Reviewing the paperwork in her hands, she said, "Your blood work doesn't look bad, except your liver enzymes are elevated. How much alcohol do you drink, Michael?" More serious face on now.

"A couple of drinks a day," Michael replied sleepily.

"Well, you should definitely cut back. That doesn't seem to be your major problem right now, though," she said. "The good news is you won't need surgery, but the bad news is that there is a lot of free air in your abdomen, and although I think you have a severe fecal impaction (FOS again), I don't think there is anything serious going on."

Nelly

"Great," Michael replied, pretty much out of it now between his high temperature and the morphine taking hold in his system. He was in "la la land," showing minimal interest in activities surrounding him.

"That is great news," I said with a sense of relief. I was willing Michael to jump off the table and get back home where we could get a few hours of rest before the "rat" woke up and demanded attention, and my work day began. My mind had already switched out of the danger mode to all the things I had to get done the next day on minimal, if any, sleep.

"Well, I just want to make sure I'm not missing anything, so I'm going to call in Dr. Gorge, a surgeon on call, just to look at the CT scan with another set of eyes. Even though it's three in the morning, I want to make sure I'm reading things correctly, since there isn't a radiologist here to read the scan."

I was ready to bolt out the door, family in tow, thinking we were one step ahead of the game, and now I had to take another step back and continue to sit and wait for another opinion, my back aching from the perch atop the swivel chair.

Even though moments before I was deeply concerned, now my thoughts went to the full day ahead of activities. I was beginning to get indignant that Michael was peacefully snoring away on the ER bed while I was doing the waiting and taking care of the baby, who had suddenly woken up needing a bottle and a change.

After getting Janelle settled back in her infant seat to snooze, a man whom I assumed to be Dr. Gorge came teetering through the door. He was about sixty years old and had a slightly bent five-feet-nine frame. His eyeglasses sat half-way down his nose, and he had a balding, grey hairline. He seemed pretty alert, with razor-sharp, beady eyes scanning and assessing the patient and the two of us parked in the corner. He didn't appear perturbed at all at being awakened from the night's slumber. I'm sure after years of the on-call schedule a person gets used to a disruptive life.

Closely on the doc's shirttails were a couple ER nurses and the original young ER doc, all floating into the room and surrounding a sleeping Michael. One nurse began to work on Michael, establishing another IV line, and several small pouches of IV fluids were placed on the poles above the main lines. The piggy-backed small pouches of fluids were opened to begin flowing into Michael's system rapidly. I surmised they were antibiotics.. Michael slowly opened his eyes with all the commotion.

Dr. Gorge shook Michael's hand, and without mincing words, the straight-shooter professional began: "You are a mighty sick young man, fella. I reviewed the CT results, and it looks like you perforated your bowel. There are all kinds of toxins floating through your system right now. I'm going to have to take you to surgery to take out any diseased bowel. You'll more than likely end up with a temporary colostomy, where you'll defecate through a pouch in the side of your abdomen. After three months, we'll try to reverse the colostomy, hook up all the plumbing, and see if things work. If things don't work, you'll have a colostomy for the rest of your life. In the meantime, we'll be pumping you full of antibiotics to try to kill all the toxins. We need to get you ready for surgery and operate as soon as possible. Any questions?"

Michael, not knowing if he was on foot or horseback at that moment in time, nodded his head in agreement to whatever was being said and fell back into a snoring slumber.

I knew full well what the doc had just said, and I was filled with dread—not so much for myself and Janelle, because I believed Michael would be okay physically. He was a tough man. I was upset for Michael, who was a very private and dignified man at the age of forty. I knew living with a colostomy for the rest of his life would virtually kill him.

Before Dr. Gorge went to get scrubbed in for the OR, he turned to me and glanced down at the sleeping baby moving her jaw and mouth in her sleep like she was still suckling. His face softened.

"If you hadn't gotten your husband in tonight or had I not been called," he said softly, "your husband would most likely been dead by tomorrow. Good job, Mom!" With a twitch of his hardened lips, he bolted out the door to do battle against Michael's diseased bowel. They wheeled Michael into the OR, and as the doors were closing I heard George Thorogood's "Bad to the Bone" piped through the surgical suite. Somehow I knew Michael would be just fine in this surgeon's skillful hands!

Michael made it through two grueling major surgeries and lived with a colostomy for three months. Luckily, the colostomy was able to be reversed. Unfortunately, Atty, who was now fourteen, didn't fare as well. As Michael went into the hospital for his second surgery, I had Atty put to sleep. It was devastating to both of us, as she had been our first baby and Michael's closest friend in the world.

Shortly after Michael's crisis passed, I was sitting at my desk one sunny day and received a phone call from the front desk operator. "There is a Helen on the line for you," the nasal operator said.

"Oh, super, put her through," I said.

Helen was an old neighbor from my childhood and my father's common-law wife. They re-connected after Boom-boom but never got married. They had been together for fourteen years or so. They were planning to visit Wisconsin from Arizona in a couple weeks, so I thought maybe Helen was calling to get specific directions to the new house we had moved into.

"Hi, honey," Helen said softly. "Is there anyone there with you now?"

"No, I'm just getting work done at my desk," I said cheerily, as I had accomplished a lot of work in my half day already. "Are you guys still planning to come?"

Helen, now sniffling, hesitated into the receiver. "I don't know how to tell you this, but Dad died last night."

"What?" I said, not understanding the words just spoken.

"I'm so sorry, honey, but your dad was sick, and he didn't want to tell you. He was diagnosed with lung cancer several months ago and was undergoing radiation. He had his last treatment yesterday. He was really tired and went to bed. He asked for a chocolate shake, drank half of it, went to sleep, and never woke up. I tried to get him to tell you he was sick, but he didn't want you to worry with all the stuff going on in your life. He said he would beat this cancer, because he wanted to see more of his only granddaughter growing up. I'm so sorry."

I was in a state of shock. Instead of planning for a visit, we needed to plan a funeral. Helen and I talked through the mechanics of things. Dad wanted to be cremated. Living in Arizona and not married to Helen, they required my sister's and my signatures as the next of kin on the cremation papers that would be faxed to me shortly.

I called Michael first, and then dialed Susie's work number. I got the company operator and asked for my sister, stating that it was an emergency.

"What happened?" Susie came on line after a lengthy hold. She sounded harried, and her voice was laced with concern.

"Dad died last night." I briefly summarized the circumstances relayed by Helen moments earlier.

"Oh, thank God, I thought something happened to John! You don't know how you scared me!" She was berating me for scaring her, and I had just told her that her father was dead! Weird reaction.

John was Susie's husband and was severely diabetic. In the past he had become hypoglycemic and fallen into coma-like states, sometimes finding himself off road in a ditch somewhere, so Susie's concern for John was absolutely legitimate. I thought that it was an odd response after finding out your father was dead, though. I knew there had been no love lost between my sister and our dad. Since childhood, Susie never liked our father, often telling our mom to leave him. Given our father's record of destruction, I could understand her indignation. With Michael encouraging me along the way, I had become close to my father again and tended to overlook his personal proclivities and accept him for who he was. At a moment like this, I was glad I had a good relationship with him.

We had a memorial service for my dad. I saw Jeffry. I drank. Lots.

A few months later, I needed a break, so my mom came to babysit Janelle. Michael and I were invited to another of our neighbor's children's weddings. Being a good Catholic family, they had nine kids, and we were coming up on wedding number five or six shortly.

I was walking in the mall with my typical mom uniform—jeans, sneakers, and a UW-Eau Claire sweatshirt, with remnants of spit-up on the sweatshirt dulled by multiple washings. My hair traveled down my back in a French braid, and I looked pretty decent from the neck up! All I needed was an outfit to wear. I found shoes I liked, and like many other mall patrons I was marching hurriedly down the causeway with a handled package in tow.

I entered Gantos, a woman's specialty store, where they had reasonably priced items that may be appropriate wedding attire. After shopping a short time, I had five or six items I wanted to try on. The dressing rooms were to the right of the store as you entered. Many of the clothes were on tall racks at head level or above, lining the view to the dressing rooms. The dressing rooms were very private, and it appeared no one was in any of the them as I walked down the dim hall. I entered a dressing room near the far end, flipped the outside door tag indicating it was occupied, and shut the door to get down to business. The doors were magnetized with no locks. The dressing rooms were small, and there was one elongated beveled mirror in the corner. I tried on multiple clothing items and saved my favorite for last.

It was a fancy pant suit, all one item. The bottoms were black, and the leg line flowed nicely. The top was ivory in color with a sheer bodice of black above the breast area and down the sleeves. It had a zippered back and a thick black belt to cinch my small waist. It was satin material with a flowing leg line, so it looked fancy enough to wear to a nice wedding yet was a simple design, which I tended to favor. Due to the sheer bodice, I decided to shed my bra so I could try it on without straps interrupting the view.

I liked the reflection of what I saw when I was zipped and belted in. A quick decision- maker by nature, I decided this was "it." As I undressed and stripped down to thong undies, I bent over to pick my matching lace bra off the floor. Near the corner of the dressing room where the beveled mirror was placed, I retrieved my undergarment and then saw ... *a contorted face!*

"Oh my God!" I said, more surprised than anything. Quickly, my brain synthesized that it had to be a small child crawling around under the dressing room openings, as only a small child could fit that low, about a foot off the ground. I grabbed whatever clothing I could find off the floor to cover my bare breasts and angled down to look for the child. As I looked underneath the opening into the dressing room adjacent to mine, I saw a fully-grown man lying on his side on the floor with his foot propped against his dressing room door so no one would enter. He was in the process of jacking off.

I stood immediately, saying "Oh ... my ... God" much louder this time as I grabbed more clothing to cover up. I instinctively pressed my back against my dressing room door to divert his intrusion. As I did so, I heard the rustling of clothing, a quick zip up, and the opening and slamming shut of the magnetized door next to mine as the loser ran away. It took several moments to even process what had happened. I got dressed mechanically as my mind tried to wrap itself around what it had just seen.

I approached the sales clerk behind the cash register and must have looked a shade of green. I felt like I could puke. Clinging to the pant suit in my arms like it was a lifeline (after all, I was still going to purchase the outfit), I looked at the nicely dressed, young sales clerk behind the counter and said; "I think you have a problem here!" I proceeded to explain what had just taken place.

The store staff immediately called mall security, and— wouldn't you know it— my Paul Blart to the rescue happened to be a high school classmate. Just my luck. I had to relive the incident and embarrassingly tell the story to someone who knew me. Security went after the man and was able to follow the perp as he left the mall though a side entrance. Unfortunately, mall security is not able to do anything other than follow a suspect and alert appropriate officials.

Waiting to hear back from mall security, I was stationed back at the "scene of the crime," talking to the sales clerks. They knew the guy.

"Yeah, he was always in here shopping for his girlfriend," one clerk innocently said. "But he never bought anything. He must have been doing this for months … sneaking back there. We'd have no idea anything was going on."

As per usual, Michael was traveling for work—somewhere in Texas that week. Whenever I needed Michael the most, he seemed to be absent. I entered the house and sent the babysitter on her way. I made a couple of strong drinks to calm shattered nerves. Around 8:30 p.m., I got a phone call from the local police. I needed to come down to the station, as they had a possible suspect in custody and needed someone to positively identify him.

Packing up Janelle and calling a good friend from work for fortification, we went down to the police station. Thank God my girlfriend, Teri, was with me. Walking into a police station at night in the dark with all that testosterone flowing was not fun. The policemen looked me up and down, and I felt as though they were as lecherous as the guy they were detaining. One nice officer sat me down and gave me a photo line-up of six men who looked similar to one another. He asked me if it would help me identify the guy if I re-enacted the scene, and he put the pictures of the faces on the floor. Somehow, I didn't find that funny and wanted out of there quickly! I picked out the offender immediately.

After I identified the guy, they had me look at him in a room with a one-way mirror. Even though it made me sick to my stomach to look at him, I forced myself to do it. It was him, still dressed in his getaway faded denim jeans, a white polo shirt tucked in to belted pants. He

145

looked like your typical "boy on campus." All American, dark haired, quite handsome, well dressed, and clean. Not anyone I would pick out as the slime he was.

Apparently, the offender had been engaged in this "activity" for eight months or so, according to what the clerks at the store and the police could figure out. He had also flashed himself to a woman sunbathing by her pool the previous summer. The cops said he had a girlfriend, and after talking to her and searching the couple's apartment, the cops concluded they were into really kinky sexual things. I didn't doubt them for a minute.

Michael flew home to be with me as soon as he could get a flight out of Texas. By the time he got home, the incident was in the paper and on the news. My fifteen minutes of fame.

Not only was this year one of the best by having Janelle, it also was one of the worst. The month of March in Wisconsin is often known as the month of weather that comes in like a lion and leaves like a lamb, or vice versa. That is how 1997 felt to me. It started like a lamb with the birth of Janelle, and left like a lion, mighty and roaring as it went. After throwing in a couple of car accidents toward the end (surprising that neither of them were my fault), the year was complete. In summary, it was one chaotic event after the next. When the trauma of one life event settled down, it seemed like the curve balls kept coming. I was barely able to hang on to the mitt as the balls kept flying my way.

CHAPTER 25

MORE DRAMA

Things were status quo for the next few years. Michael and I continued maintaining a facade of normalcy. I would go on drinking binges when it fit into my schedule, and Michael drank alcohol daily. Both of us hid bottles, and it became a game for me to try to find where he was hiding his bottle ... usually blackberry brandy in a paper bag. He would have a bottle ready as soon as he got done with work, and imbibe on the commute home, hiding his liquor in the garage before entering the house. His routine was work hard, hit the bottle, and sleep. Get up the next day and repeat.

I would have my stash of alcohol hidden whenever I decided to go on a binge. My drinking was a vicious cycle. A break in calendar events where there were no meetings, volunteer obligations, or various lessons for Janelle would begin my spree. I would start drinking in the morning and alternate drinking with napping in sync with Janelle's timetable.

When it was time to get back to reality, I would sober up. Sobering up would entail a dismal night of sweating, shaking, and insomnia as my system tried to rid itself of the poison. I would re-engage in life and be abstinent until the next time I had a schedule break. There was always something that would happen—usually some emotional event, either real or perceived, and I would begin the drinking cycle once more. I would binge drink about every month or two. It was a Ferris wheel ride that never stopped.

It was no way to live, but I didn't know how to live differently. At times I was so sick; I would end up puking my guts out. First bile would rise, and then dry heaves would ravish my body. At times my liver actually throbbed in protest. I knew I was slowly killing myself. I had been self-destructive for so long, I couldn't stop. I was miserable, Glinda was thriving.

The thing about a brain disease is that the brain protects its diseased state. Glinda convinced me that I didn't have a problem. After all, I had no trouble avoiding alcohol during my pregnancy. That must prove something, right? I could quit drinking for months at a time. People with real drinking problems drank daily, like Michael. Right?

After quitting a boozing cycle, I always swore to myself it would be the last. I always started drinking again. Even though deep down I knew I had a problem, I didn't know what to do about it. Although never suicidal, I thought it would be easier not to wake up during these dark days with clinical depression dancing around me. I felt as though I was in a deep, dark hole and couldn't find my way to the surface. I was going through the motions in life, but not really living.

Early one morning, I found a mouse trapped in our large ceramic kitchen sink, trying desperately to claw its way out of the basin. I watched for a few moments as this creature repeatedly made its way from one side to another, looking for a means of escape. I peered at the miniature rat as he became more frenzied by the second until finally, taking pity on the rodent, I said out loud, "I know how you feel, little guy." I felt as frightened and trapped in my life as he must have felt. I donned a pair of work gloves and gingerly lifted him out of the sink and watched him scurry away, thankfully, to the safety of prairie grass out our back door.

nelly

The deeper I got into my addiction, the more I hated myself. I prayed someone would come and lift me out of my valley and set me free, as I had the small, grey mammal. No one came. Janelle always snapped me out of my spells. If not for myself, I needed to live for her.

During this period of time, I sought help from any professional I could. I had been diagnosed as having clinical depression and various other disorders straight out of the *DSM* (Diagnostic and Statistical Manual of Mental Disorders) *Manual*. I tried medicinal cocktails of various sizes, and different colors of pills for whatever disorder was freshly diagnosed. Nothing seemed to work. I was drowning and didn't know how to get to the surface for sweet air.

Unfortunately, I was never honest about my drinking binges with any clinician. I would lie, downplay, or pass over the question of substance abuse, until one astute clinician thought it might be wise to have me take an alcohol assessment. It was a diagnostic tool, she said, to rule out any problem with alcohol. Surprisingly, I was able to be honest on the test, whereas I couldn't be with any clinician. Maybe my perfectionistic upbringing came into play. I was compelled to ace any exam!

The results were not surprising. The middle-aged clinician administering the test looked me directly in the eye and said through a smoker's raspy voice, "You came out high on the scale for drinking alcohol. I would advise you enter outpatient treatment." Her tone was non-compassionate, matter-of-fact. She had a challenging timbre to her voice. I stared at the woman in disbelief for perhaps a full minute, not saying a word. She stared back and didn't back down. I detested the woman. She was delivering news that I knew to be true, yet was not willing or able to acknowledge. I immediately went on the defensive.

I looked at her lined, rugged face and said, "Well, that is fine and dandy, but I have a three-year-old at home, and I'm the only one able to care for her, so entering treatment is not an option for me." I went on to tell this woman that alcohol wasn't my problem. *If Michael would help me with our daughter … if I wasn't responsible for everything around the house … if Michael didn't drink so much … if I didn't have a stressful job … if life would stop dealing me blows … then I would and could be happy.* I felt obliged to blame others for my problems, unwilling to look at my part in the dysfunction that was my life. After all, no one was putting the bottle to my head and pulling the trigger, except me. It was like I was standing in a burning house, only needing to take a step or two to get out of the fire, yet I chose to remain and get burned. And get burned I did.

After that assessment, I swore off going to any more professionals and kept limping forward as best I could. I didn't mention the assessment to Michael, and went on living a smoldering existence.

One Monday morning I got a call from Susie's husband, John. It was mid-summer after the Fourth of July holiday.

"I don't know what to do with Susie," John said with desperation in his voice. "She's acting strangely, and I was wondering if you could come over and talk to her."

By this point we were living fifteen minutes from my sister, yet we didn't see each other except on holidays and the odd occasion. We were both busy in our own lives. I was trying to hang on to a job and a marriage while raising a small child—juggling all of life's balls in the air on unsteady feet. Susie's lifestyle with John was living as DINCs (Dual Income, No Children). They lived "the American dream" and spent time traveling, golfing, and relaxing at their summer home on a lake in Northern Wisconsin.

As I pulled up to their sprawling brick ranch, John bolted down the front steps to meet me in the driveway.

"So what's going on?" I asked, rather nonchalantly.

John leaned into my open car window. "Well, your sister started acting peculiar a few days ago. She alternates between being really tired, and not being able to sit still. Today she started to pace around the house, and I couldn't get her to stop. She's also acting really paranoid and is talking about people at work being out to get her! She keeps saying that I'm having an affair with this waitress we know from the country club, and she talks about my plan to commit suicide."

John looked me squarely in the eye. "I swear on the Bible, nothing is going on between me and anyone else, and I certainly am not going to kill myself! I don't know what to do anymore. I try to talk logically to her, but she just doesn't listen. You have to help me!"

"Wow!" I said both shock and disbelief lining my response. "It sounds like she should be in a hospital, for God's sake! I just talked to Susie on the phone last week, and she sounded completely normal, offering to drop off some clothes she wanted me to have." I couldn't wrap my head around John's description of my sister. I'd never witnessed any of the behavior he was now relating.

I quickly transformed into nurse mode and began to drill John with questions. "When exactly did the symptoms start? Has she been doing anything out of the ordinary? Has this ever happened before? Does anything seem to make her feel better? Did she start taking any new medications or eat something out of the ordinary? Did anything unusual happen lately, at work, or between the two of you?"

"I've been racking my brain. Nothing that I can think of," he replied, desperation very close to the surface.

"Well, let me go talk to her and see for myself."

Entering their polished, recently redecorated home, I found Susie standing in the kitchen, gazing out the back door onto their expansive cedar deck. She was mumbling to herself words I couldn't decipher. My sister's usual flawless appearance was disheveled. She had on a stained, old, grey and red crocheted sweater she hugged close to her body, despite the summer high temperatures. Mismatched blue shorts clung to her rather bountiful lower half. John always ironed Susie's shorts, but today they looked like the body of a Shar Pei, wrinkles everywhere.

"Hi Susie," I said in a chipper voice. "I was out getting groceries, so I thought I'd stop by and say hi first." I didn't want to let on that John had called me.

Susie did a slow turn away from the pristine window, and with a wrinkled brow said in a monotone voice: "How come you're here?"

I repeated my reason for stopping by.

"I don't believe you," Susie said. Then she let out a long, slow sigh, and began pacing back and forth in front of the French patio doors, hugging herself continually.

Their house was laid out in a circular pattern, from their elegant formal living room to the large, homey kitchen, charming eating area, and back into the living room. There was a wall of stone for a dual access fireplace in between the living areas.

I began to walk next to Susie, letting her set the pace for whatever mission she was on. My first clinical assessment was that there was definitely something organically wrong. She was not acting in a way I had ever seen before. "So, how have you been?" I asked, as if it were completely normal to be walking in circles in her house, chattering away.

Very matter-of-factly and conversing with a flat affect, she announced: "Bad ... John is going to leave me. He met a girl at the country club named Katie, and he's having an affair. She's blonde and skinny. It's been going on for months now. There's a book under my bed where I have everything listed. I've made note of all the plots." Susie stopped walking long enough to face me. Eyes darting all around, she whispered in my ear softly: "Your name isn't on the list."

I told her I was glad to hear that I wasn't part of the conspiracy to do her in, but quickly assured her that John was a stellar husband and not having an affair. This was a man who was as solid as a rock—church council president and very involved in the community. Such things were not in his nature, at least to my knowledge. My words fell on deaf ears, and Susie's mood went from conspiratorial to exhausted in a split second. She plopped down on her living room couch, curled up in a ball, and closed her eyes like she was about to fall asleep, indicating to me that the conversation was over.

I left my sister curled up like a cat and found John puttering in the garage. He stopped sweeping out their dog kennel long enough to ask what I thought.

"There is definitely something wrong with her," I said bluntly. "There isn't anything you can think of that has happened lately to cause such a drastic change?"

"No, nothing I can think of." John paused, shaking his head back and forth.

"I'd suggest you get her to a doctor to see what's wrong with her," I said as a clinical recommendation.

"I think maybe she just needs rest. She hasn't slept at all for several nights," John said, clearly unable to consider there was anything psychologically wrong with his wife, whom he cherished. "Could you watch her during the day this week while I'm at work, and we can see if she gets better? If she doesn't get back to normal, I'll take her to the doctor."

I agreed and said I'd be back with Janelle in the morning, but I insisted that if she wasn't getting better in a few days, we really needed to get her evaluated. I was very concerned about the behavioral transformation. John agreed and off I went to get ready to move in and babysit my older sister.

Janelle and I went to Susie's house the next morning. Although she didn't seem any worse, she certainly wasn't much improved. She would have lucid moments throughout the day, but would fall into the paranoid behavior intermingled with the high and low energy levels. During her coherent moments, I'd try to query what was going on with her. One moment she talked about our mom traveling out west (which was accurate), and the next minute she'd be crying about John's (imagined) affair. It was all very strange.

After several days of this emotional roller coaster and not seeing significant improvement, I urged John to seek professional help. So the three of us—John, Susie, and I—hurried off to a psychiatrist's office and upon his recommendation registered my sister in a local psychiatric hospital.

I was surprised Susie was willing to be admitted to the hospital. I think she was mentally and physically exhausted. I sat with John and Susie for the intake assessment, and my sister was so paranoid at that point that she thought I was actually there to do her harm. I will never forget the look she gave me. I sat across the room from her, and she looked at me like I was an alien. It pained me to have lost her trust, even though I knew it was her own mental instability driving her current delusions.

After my sister was settled in the hospital, John and I both went home for a quick reprieve before heading back later that evening for a brief visit. My sister had been given some strong medications and was sleeping soundly for the first time in quite some time. We were turned away by the hospital staff and said our farewells. They assured us they would call if we were needed.

Walking side by side to the parking lot, I looked up and saw that John had tears moving slowly down his face. He was gently shaking his head side to side and murmuring repeatedly, "I never thought it would come to this!" Lost in my own melancholy about the experience, I really didn't pay attention or discern what his remark meant. He appeared completely disoriented. I placed my arm around John's waist. We both felt a sense of relief to have Susie hospitalized, but it was bittersweet. It is grueling to watch someone you love struggle with psychoses and not be able to understand or alleviate the cause.

After a week of treatment, which involved further evaluation, medications, and much needed rest, Susie came home restored basically to normal. It was such a relief. I was never able to determine what caused my sister's temporary insanity. Once she was hospitalized, I retreated home and resumed my life's routine. I stayed in touch with John, who said Susie was improving daily, but offered little insight into the bizarre incident.

Nelly

Our mother blew into town after her vacation travels. It was toward the end of Susie's hospital stay, and by the time she saw my sister, things had stabilized. I thanked God, because Georgia would not have been able to handle Susie's temporary escape to insanity. Of course, once the crisis with my sister had passed, I coped the only way I knew how. I went on a drinking binge as soon as I could. I needed to soothe my frayed nerves and emotions.

Strangely, the episode with my sister was never discussed again. My sister told me months later she had to start drinking decaffeinated coffee, and that her lunacy was due to her being overly caffeinated. Okay.

With life back on solid ground, my new desire to stir the pot morphed into wanting another child. Janelle was around four years of age and needed a sibling. Wanting another child consumed me like wild fires engulfing a dried plain. There was one problem. After delivering Janelle, I went into menopause. I was thirty-seven years old. The only thing that made sense to me was that Michael and I needed to start an adoption process. Michael didn't want to. I was insistent. Then Michael came home one day and said he had received an offer to interview for the position of president of a financial company in Nebraska. He got the job, so we moved.

Michael went to Nebraska ahead of us and bought a house. After closing on the house, I saw it for the first time. Turning right from 180th street, Michael, Janelle, and I wound up a hill into a neighborhood whose large posted sign announced we were entering "The Ridges." The entryway into the subdivision had waterfalls and geese sculptures. As we drove down the main route, I noticed that residential areas off the lane appeared to be gated communities. Cherry blossom trees lined the boulevard, and the grass looked as green as emeralds interspersed with winding streets and hills. This area was nothing like I had envisioned. I was anticipating farm fields, cows, and flat lands. I was wrong.

Michael wasn't sure if he was driving in the direction of our new house, as the neighborhoods all looked similar and were arranged in pods of expansive homes. Eventually, we found our way and pulled cautiously into the driveway of our new abode.

I saw rose-colored siding with blue shuttered windows and red brick half way up a two-story home. I had seen pictures Michael had sent of the house, so I knew there were five bedrooms and five bathrooms, along with the standard kitchen, living room, and formal dining room. The house had a second full kitchen in the finished basement with sliding glass doors opening to ground level. The back yard butted up against a golf course. Across the fairway, mansions lined the view. Someone had recently painted the entire residence. Each room was sterile white. The house was like a blank canvas ready to have our family paint new life into it.

We quickly got acclimated to our new surroundings, and Janelle staked claim on the bedroom adjacent to ours on the upper floor. There was plenty of living space for three people. Of course, I hadn't given up the thought of adding to our family unit, and as I toured our new quarters, my thoughts circled back to promoting the idea of having more children.

Michael kept doubling his salary with every job change. The plan was for me to stay home and raise Janelle and get us settled into a new life in Nebraska, away from all things familiar and our extended family.

Continuing on my quest to have another child, I found a local organization called Nebraska Children's Home (NCH). I found out that the agency was unique in that it operated on donations alone. If chosen as an adoptive family, it cost nothing to adopt a child. After having many friends who had gone through the adoption process, I knew it could cost up to $20,000 a child or more. At NCH, adoption was gratis. Of course, as with other agencies, the family had to go through the same stringent process to be accepted as an adoptive family.

Learning of the free adoption service, I just knew God had sent us here for this reason alone. Why else would we have been given this opportunity? A higher purpose had to be in play for us to be called away from Wisconsin to Nebraska, for goodness' sake. Here it was staring me in the face. We were going to be blessed with another child! I convinced myself this was reality.

There was one problem. Michael didn't want to adopt a child. He was happy with one healthy child and didn't want to push our luck by getting into a circumstance that had the potential to be sub-optimal in his mind. I was impervious to his concerns and blocked his protests, moving full steam ahead with or without him. I attended meetings, picked up the application, and finally, after much consternation, drama, and threats on my part, Michael relented. We went through the adoption process and were approved.

If you looked at our family from the outside, the pretense was handsome. Two polished, educated, good looking people with a healthy daughter, making all the right moves. We were financially stable and living in a big house in the posh part of the city. We had friends, were active in church and the community, were members of the country club, and were very involved in neighborhood activities and functions. The disguise was firmly in place.

Behind closed doors, the atmosphere was tense and definitely unhealthy. We were a married couple, but each of us was very much living alone, lost in our own afflictions. It was a dysfunctional household masquerading as normal. Each day was a new flip of the coin—heads one day, and tails the next. I felt as if we were walking on a tightrope, presenting one face to the outside world, but living another. I was bracing myself every day for the long fall.

The adoption agency social worker guaranteed we would get a child … it was just a matter of time. They said it could take up to two years. I was now forty-three and Michael was forty-five. I kept honing in on the Hollywood stars who were having children later in life and thinking to myself that if they could do it, so could I. Janelle deserved to have a sibling. As usual, I felt compelled to do parenthood perfectly, which in my mind required a house with two children.

By October 2003, the law required that we renew our paperwork with the adoption agency. We had started the adoption process a year earlier and had been on the waiting list for eight months by the time we were approved. Michael put his foot down. No more. He wasn't interested in continuing with the adoption process. He said he was getting too old. He didn't want to be a grandfather-aged person at his kid's high school graduation. Janelle was enough for him. We had gone through the process and hadn't been chosen as an adoptive family in eight months. According to Michael, we made the attempt to add to our family, but it wasn't meant to be. He accepted that fact readily. I didn't.

I knew I was at the end. My vision for our family was shattered in a million pieces like splintered glass. I was angry and resentful toward Michael for not supporting my dream. I mushroomed into even more of an emotional wreck. I hit the bottle harder than ever.

And then came The Fall.

CHAPTER 26

THE FALL

Eight o'clock in the morning, and I was dialing the phone in slow motion. Each number pressed tore a piece of my heart away. Asking for Elaine, the case worker at Nebraska Children's Home, cued a lump to form in my throat, and I didn't know if I'd be able to get words out.

"Hi, Elaine, this is Nelly Branson. You need to withdraw our adoption application. Michael had decided he doesn't want to renew our paperwork." I broke down in sobs and could no longer speak. Silence stretched out. I could tell I caught Elaine completely off guard.

"I'm so sorry to hear that," Elaine said regretfully. She was our behind-the-scenes cheerleader throughout the adoption process. She was hoping to be able to place a child in our home.

I managed to creak out, "Thanks for everything you've done. I have to go now. I'm pretty upset."

"Good luck to you and your family. I've enjoyed working with you," she said with remorse.

Hanging up the phone felt like letting go of a lifeline. My dream evaporated before my eyes, and I was forced to grieve its loss. Despite the early hour, I turned for solace in my oldest friend, the bottle.

At this point in my drinking, I would consume whatever was in the house. Bottle of wine, beer, hard liquor—it didn't matter. I drank to numb the pain. I would mix whiskey with root beer if that was all there was in the liquor cabinet. It didn't matter how it tasted. I would plug my nose and gulp down the alcohol until I felt the familiar warmth spread through my veins and settle me down. It was like covering up in a heated blanket after exposure to winter's icy embrace, only the alcohol warmed me from the inside out.

This particular day, I decided I would drink until I could fall asleep. I was emotionally destroyed. My plan was to drink and get a nap in before school ended. That way I would be semi-functional when Janelle came home. My plan didn't work.

The more alcohol I drank, the less sedated I felt. Instead, my anxiety was amplified to the point where I could not stay still for long. It felt like my body no longer belonged to me. My brain would say "settle down and relax," but my body couldn't do it. So I drank more, and the anxiety intensified.

At 10:00 a.m. I called Michael at work and told him he had to come home, as I wasn't doing well. He must have been able to hear the instability in my voice.

"I'll be right home," he said. He had a half hour commute home from work, and during that time I drank, cried, and paced back and forth in front of our plantain shutters, praying for Michael's maroon Lexus to show up in the driveway.

Michael walked through the door in his pressed business suit. Before he got too far in the house, I screamed at him.

"I need help. There is something wrong with me. I can't relax or stop myself from pacing."

"What should I do?" he asked, completely at a loss of how to help his crazed wife.

"Call my doctor and tell her what's wrong. She'll refer us somewhere," I said, desperate for someone other than myself to take charge of the situation.

Nelly

Michael made phone calls and we ended up in the ER at a local hospital. I couldn't stop crying or pacing in the small ER room. I felt like a caged animal with no escape in sight. Michael would make comments like, "It's a seventy-degree sunny day out, and we're sitting here in the ER like this?" I'm sure his intentions were to point out that I should be grateful for a beautiful day, but his words had the opposite effect on me, and I cried harder. I felt like I was breaking inside and all he could do was blame me for acting crazy on a day when we could be enjoying the sunshine and warmth. I not only felt crazy ... I felt like a burden.

Nothing he could say or do would soothe me. After all, it was his fault that I was in this position. If he hadn't put his foot down about the adoption, none of this would have happened. It was his responsibility I was in this emotional state, and I despised him for it. I unfairly blamed him for everything.

I was processed through a medical evaluation. My blood alcohol level came back extremely elevated, which obviously was no shock to anyone, except me. I told the nursing staff and doctor I had only consumed half a bottle of wine that morning. Yeah, right! After the medical professionals were done with me, there was some new lady assigned to my case. The lady was probably a hospital social worker. Through sobbing and tears, I told her the long, sordid story of how I ended up in the ER.

The woman was middle-aged, nicely dressed, and had the aura of the person that did the alcohol assessment on me years ago. Only this woman had more of a compassionate side. When she asked Michael questions, he just shrugged his shoulders and clearly did not want anything to do with the mess of a woman in front of him—his crumbling wife. Who could blame him, really? It had to be an ugly sight.

After a lengthy evaluation, the woman told me there were no beds available in the hospital, so they would discharge me. Their explanation—I wasn't a suicidal risk, I was just psychologically ill. They felt okay releasing me to the care of Michael.

I saw my lifeline once again slipping away. I was devastated.

"I can't go on like this," I said. I never want to feel this way again. You have to tell me what to do. I'll do whatever it takes, but I can't live like this anymore! Can't you please admit me?"

The woman outlined a discharge plan for me, which entailed me going the very next day to Michael's Employee Assistance Program (EAP) for a thorough evaluation. The appointment was already made. All I had to do was show up.

"Don't think about anything other than this first step," she said kindly. "All you have to do is show up at this appointment tomorrow. Don't think beyond that point."

For whatever reason, that statement resonated with me, and I felt a sense of calm wash over me. I didn't have to fix the world. All I had to do was show up at an appointment. Easy peasy!

After an extremely restless and sobering night, I made it to the appointment on time. My mantra was, "All I have to do is show up at the appointment. That's it." I was hanging on to that thought like a drowning person would a buoy.

The gentleman assigned to speak with me at the EAP was very nice. I'll call him Mr. Mann, as to this day I don't recall his name, other than it was a short surname. Mr. Mann came out of his small office with a big smile on his face. He was in a grey suit with a soft pink shirt. He walked swiftly to my seated position in the waiting room.

"Nelly, I am so glad to meet you," he said, shaking my hand vigorously.

I don't know what I was expecting, but this wasn't it. As morose as I was feeling, I thought that under the circumstance everyone should act as gloomy as I felt. To me, this was the beginning to an end I didn't want to acknowledge. How can anyone be happy? My world as I knew it was crumbling before me.

Ushered into his cozy office, I was immediately put at ease by this gentleman. I was asked questions and told the truth for the first time in my life. I was like a water can placed under a flowing spigot. As I began my story, the truth spilled over the edge, and the years of self-destruction lay as a puddle at my feet.

I felt safe and secure in this tiny corner of the world. Mr. Mann acted like he had all the time in the world to hear my story, and I felt as if he passed no judgment on my behavior. After listening to my diatribe, Mr. Mann recommended I undergo another alcohol assessment.

"I know I'm chemically dependent," I told him, flat out. "I know I have an addictive personality. I just don't want to be called an alcoholic."

"Then don't call yourself that ... just take this next step ... please."

I did take that next step, and the one after that. I was reminded of Janelle's first unsteady steps, wobbling and falling, trying desperately to make it to my stretched open arms as I encouraged her progress. I felt like an infant taking baby steps. For some reason, I could handle this format—just one small step at a time, with people like Mr. Mann encouraging me each step I took. It was like an invisible force took hold, and I felt a hand in mine steadying the way and propelling my movement onward.

I ranked high, once again, on drinking alcoholically (surprise, surprise), and once again was encouraged to enter outpatient treatment. This time, I agreed. With Janelle in school, I could easily start the three day a week morning treatment sessions.

After I agreed to begin treatment, I was encouraged to meet my counselor, but only if I would like to. The staff at EAP must have known what they were doing, because they were allowing me to make choices, not forcing anything on me in my fragile state of mind. Having choices along the way, no matter how small they were, gave me a comfort level in the process. I was told Dolores would be my treatment counselor.

Shortly thereafter, Dolores floated into the room. Instead of hovering over my seated position, she sat down in the chair next to me and placed her hand on my arm. Dolores was in her fifties. She appeared to be of Native American decent and was dressed in clothes hinting at that as well. She had dark hair and the softest, brown, doe-like eyes I had ever seen. Compassion poured out of them.

"I am so glad you're taking this step," she said. "I know how scary it can be, because I was in your shoes about twenty years ago. I can promise you that you'll begin to feel a whole lot better soon. If you don't have any questions for me, I'll see you Monday morning. Feel free to call me if you have any questions between now and then. There is one rule, however—you cannot come to treatment impaired. If you drink before coming to treatment, you'll be asked to leave." She pressed her business card into my sweaty palm with her first name and inscribed phone number written in red ink.

Monday morning I was extremely nervous. I kept thinking: *How is this happening? How did I get to this point? I am a wife, a mother, a master's prepared nurse. I never had a DUI, was never in legal trouble, I live in a mansion on a golf course, I'm married to a president of a company, and I have a healthy, happy daughter. I can't actually be about to enter a treatment program! I can't be an alcoholic. No way!* Glinda was hard at work trying to protect herself.

I wanted a drink to soothe my nerves, but I was determined to follow the rules. People believed in me, taking time to help me, and I had a daughter that needed a healthy mother. The faces flashed before me—the lady in the ER, Mr. Mann, Dolores, but most importantly, Janelle. I would find the strength to meet my demons head on, no matter what it took this time. *Just one baby step at a time.*

I made sure to dress nicely—a pricey, soft, green angora sweater with tight fitting skinny black jeans and lace up boots. I wanted my appearance to say, "I'm put together, I am healthy, I don't need to be here, and I am *not* an alcoholic. I am above it all." I needed to at least look polished on the outside as my insides were decaying. Maybe putting on the expensive costume allowed me to feel somewhat in control, even though my life was spinning out of control. I entered the assigned treatment room with a protective chip on my shoulder.

Nelly

The session started promptly at 8:00 a.m. There were seven of us in the somewhat drab by, weathered room. Chairs were arranged in a circular pattern. I sat down and hugged myself, as I was feeling cold, alone, and anxious. It was apparent that I was the newcomer. Before starting, participants conversed back and forth in a friendly and jovial manner. I found out that everyone there was in a staggered part of their treatment program, so people came and went on a fluctuating basis, and the group was used to new people joining.

Dolores began by asking me to introduce myself, which I did. Everyone in unison and with enthusiasm said, "Welcome, Nelly." Dolores asked how I felt about being there.

"Scared, nervous, and I can't believe that I'm here," I said. "I'm wondering how I even got here." I responded with nervous unsteadiness in my voice, my gaze focused on an unseen lint speck on the carpeted floor. Clearly, the people in the room knew how I felt. I could sense their empathy and support.

Dolores then invited everyone to introduce themselves to me and give a short introduction. The guy next to me jumped at the chance.

"I'm Brian. I started treatment about three weeks ago. I'm a medical student, and I'm gay. I'm having trouble with my family accepting me as gay, so I got into drugs—big time."

"I'm Jessica," said the next in line in the circle. Jessica looked to be in her mid-thirties, was casually dressed, and had long, blonde, curly hair. She had green eyes under long lashes, and her friendly demeanor toward me continued with, "This is my second time in treatment. I'm a stay-at-home mom to a two-year old. I'm married, and my husband is a lawyer in town. I'm an alcoholic."

Next was Kevin, a businessman dressed in a suit. "Welcome to the group, Nelly. I'm Kevin, and I started treatment five weeks ago. I'm having marital problems. My wife and I are separated, and it's hard being away from my family and kids. I am an alcoholic."

"Hi, I'm Nancy. My four kids are all grown and out of the house. I was bored, so I developed a drinking problem. I started treatment last week." Nancy was married to a millionaire. She was petite with short grey hair and beautiful blue-grey eyes. Her lips were lined with red lip stick. She was very classy and dressed that way. I was drawn to her spunky personality immediately.

"Hi, I'm Karen. I'm also married to a lawyer and have one son. I ended up here after trying to kill myself. I drank vanilla and rubbing alcohol and ended up in the hospital with kidney failure and almost died. My mom was an alcoholic, so I guess I'm following in her footsteps."

Karen was another beauty. She had short, dark hair with blonde highlights, coiffed perfectly. She was dressed in a young, hip fashion and appeared to be in her mid-thirties as well. Deep dimples pressed into her cheeks gave her a cherubic flair. Little did I know at that point that Karen would become a life-long friend to me in this program.

After the introductions, I was much more relaxed. These people were very open about who and what they were. They didn't look embarrassed or ashamed, even though that is how I was feeling about myself sitting in that room.

Dolores summarized things nicely by saying that all of us had a different story, but a common problem. We were there to learn and help one another. My preconceived notion of "alcoholics" as stereotypical street bums with the brown paper bags and bottles vanished instantaneously. These were my people, and after the first session I felt seismic relief. It was like the last puzzle piece in a jigsaw picture snapping into place. I knew this was where I belonged.

The turnaround in my life was almost immediate. Once I was able to truly embrace the first step in the twelve-step program of recovery, my compulsion to drink alcohol miraculously dissipated. The first step states simply: We admit we were powerless over alcohol, and that our lives have become unmanageable.

For me, this was the only step of the recovery process that mattered. Once I "got it," the other steps flowed easily, and everything in my life improved. The dark clouds ebbed, and sunshine began to seep into my life.

Another amazing thing happened in treatment—I learned that alcoholism was a genetic disease, one that wasn't my fault. I was born with the predisposition to the disease. I couldn't have avoided Glinda if I'd wanted to. All the other factors in my life allowed Glinda to emerge. It wasn't my weakness; it was a genetic flaw, a defect of character of sorts. I cannot tell you how untethered I began to feel as I gained an understanding that it wasn't my fault!

For the first time in my life, I was also required to closely examine the behaviors and actions that got me to this place. I wasn't allowed to blame anyone but myself. The focus was on me—my actions, my reactions, my behavior, and my honesty.

This concept of being responsible for my own actions was something that was completely foreign to me. After all, that was not how I was raised. My parents would look outside themselves when any problems arose in their lives. I never once heard my parents say, "I'm wrong," "I'm sorry," or "I apologize" for anything. They were never wrong; they were always perfect, as we were expected to be. It was always someone else's fault if anything went wrong. It never occurred to them or to me that we were responsible for our own behavior and for the consequences of it. Such a novel thought!

I found treatment to be a priceless educational process, and I embraced the power of knowledge to conquer the demons within. Most importantly, I began to forgive and love myself. For the first time in my life, I put my own well-being above others. Over time and with the help of others suffering from this illness, I began to feel a freedom and empowerment base that couldn't be rocked. I was given a profound gift by being in treatment, something I'd lacked my entire life—coping skills.

About midway through the process, I gained the courage to tell my family—my mother and my sister—about my treatment. Both of them immediately dismissed the concept of me being alcoholic. "It's just another phase Nelly's going through," they reasoned. Thus, we never discussed it.

Michael, on the other hand, although somewhat skeptical at first, could see the change in my behavior and seemed to accept my illness with minimal consternation. He was okay with everything ... as long as it didn't affect his drinking.

CHAPTER 27

SOBRIETY

Over the next three years, I blossomed. Looking back now, I'd say I grew up. I was no longer that small frightened child or stunted, damaged teenager. I was like a tulip in spring, bursting forth through the tough, cracked soil and burgeoning into a colorful flower. I became an adult and began acting like one.

After "graduating" from treatment, I was encouraged to participate in an after-care program, which I did. There were two additional requirements to graduate—I had to find a sponsor, and I had to attend AA meetings. Since I hadn't been led astray thus far by listening to those around me, I hastily met those two requirements.

My friend Karen, from treatment, recommended a woman's AA group. One day toward the end of treatment, she invited me to join her at the next Saturday meeting. I was scared shitless. Being in the safe cocoon of treatment was one thing, but venturing forth into the community of recovering alcoholics was quite another. Knowing that Karen would be there gave me the courage I needed to attend.

I arrived at the Presbyterian Church on my usual punctual note. I entered the building and followed directions to the downstairs labyrinth of painted cement block hallways. Someone who was very artistic had begun painting the great stories of the Bible on both sides of the lower level walls. Adam and Eve in the Garden of Eden began my journey toward the targeted room, C607. Lively greens and beautiful garden flowers jumped out of the wall while an ugly serpent was hidden, yet somehow prominent, in the picture. Noah's great ark of brown, planked wood and two of each animal pulled me further down the passageway toward my destination. The grey stone tablets of the Ten Commandments braced to fall at my feet as I passed their pronounced chiseled verbiage. Big waves and grey-black clouds looked like they would pour rain upon me at any moment as Jonah knelt in prayer from the belly of an enormous whale. Somehow passing these familiar stories silently wrapped me in comfort and propelled me forward.

As I was nearing C607, something strange happened. Freshly brewed coffee permeated the concourse. I heard boisterous voices and laughter teeming out the entryway of C607. I stopped abruptly in front of the door and re-read the numbered plaque above. I thought I must have gotten the room wrong. I had to be intruding on a church meeting, maybe a women's circle. Certainly this enthusiastic group of women could not be members of Alcoholics Anonymous.

A small group of about four women in charge of three large industrial size coffee brewers noticed me standing at the precipice with Starbucks in hand, probably looking like I was about to jump off a cliff. They waved me in, announcing in loud and proud fashion: "This is an AA meeting. Is that what you're looking for?" It was exactly what I was looking for, and something that has become a fabric of my soul ever since.

The women there embraced me, and I once again found a home. After my first soulful AA meeting, two middle-aged women came up to me and welcomed me to the group. I blurted out to the first woman I talked to, "Would you be my sponsor?" Geri had almost two years of sobriety, and she agreed. She told me she would be honored to sponsor me. Years later, I found out Geri's initial impression of me during that first meeting was that I was a "real piece of work" and in no way would I make it in the program. I must have given off the "sad sack of potatoes" vibe I was feeling that day.

Geri was a delight. She had short, red-brown hair, twinkling brown eyes, heavier set with lighter skin ... someone I would describe as a take charge "dynamo." Her Catholic Irish heritage gave her the gift of being grounded in faith with a spirited personality. Even though Geri had been in the program a short time herself, she knew all the women and was a spunky addition to the group. I always said that if I'd known these women in my drinking days, they would be a lot of fun. They were joyous and free being sober, and I desperately wanted what this group displayed.

Geri and I bonded from the first breakfast meeting we had together. She listened to my story, and I was instructed to call her every morning at 8:00 a.m. after dropping off Janelle at her elementary school. Once again, I followed instructions, and I became emotionally stronger over time. The beauty of the AA program was that I didn't have to feel alone anymore. Like a mother does with a small child, these women, and especially Geri, took me by the hand and showed me the way to an alcohol-free and fulfilling life.

When I got to my one year anniversary, I was very emotional. I had written down my thoughts so that when I got to the celebratory AA meeting, I could read them aloud instead of verbalize them on the spot. I got halfway through the first sentence and broke down sobbing, placing my head in my hands at the round table. They were tears of joy of course, because I never thought I could make a year of my life without binge drinking. As was the pattern of the past year, Geri gently nudged me and said in a quiet, solemn voice: "Here, let me help." I handed the composition over to Geri, and she began to read aloud.

> I chose December 7th as my sobriety date, because
> it was a significant date in history known as the

Japanese massacre on Pearl Harbor, a D-Day of sorts. My personal battle with alcohol and other mental illness has been an individualized D-day. Before entering this program, my "D" stood for depression, detachment, despondence, desperation, despair, dishonesty, and dreadfulness. After a year in the program, my life has transformed into a decent, delightful, and deserving existence. I owe all my thanks to the women in this room, who have taught me so much. I especially want to thank my sponsor, Geri, who has helped me navigate through the rough seas of the previous year. I love you all!

There is a product on the market called the Magic Eraser that will make scuff marks on walls magically disappear. That product is what this program has done for me and my life. Through the process of recovery, I have begun to remove the scuff marks of my life and have begun to feel like a whole, unblemished person once again ...

By the end of the essay, there wasn't a dry eye in the room. Each woman could understand and feel the sorrow, pain, and triumph that had been my first sober year.

I continued over the next two years to learn, grow, and mature in the AA program. As I did, my concern for Michael, his drinking, his well-being, and our life together as a family skyrocketed.

CHAPTER 28

ALCOHOLISM: A FAMILY DISEASE

After another two years of getting my life back on track, Geri encouraged me to start attending Al-Anon meetings in order to deal with living with an active alcoholic spouse. I thought my life had boiled down to nothing but attending meetings. Once again, I was humble and willing to listen to others wiser than myself, and I executed what was suggested.

The truth was my life was becoming more balanced. I began a jogging program, which became my new addiction, although this addiction did not damage or interfere with life. I went to one AA meeting a week, one Al-Anon meeting a week, and jogged five days a week. That became my recipe for continued personal success.

Through Al-Anon, I learned that there are only two ways to deal with an active alcoholic—what I was currently doing, which was detaching myself from Michael and living my own life, or staging an intervention. I started with the detachment approach first. I left Michael and his drinking alone. I never once asked him to quit, or even mentioned the fact that we had a wealth of beer and booze stored in the house. I never showed the slightest hesitation to entertain his work cohorts or have neighbors over and serve alcoholic beverages of all kinds. I left Michael alone and concentrated on myself and our daughter. I lived the concept of "detach with love," as Al-Anon had taught me.

I don't want to make this sound easy. It wasn't. Living with an active alcoholic is like being perched on railroad tracks with a freight train bearing down on you. I never knew which person was going to be walking through the door to our home after work. On most days, Michael would breeze through the house, blackberry brandy wafting in the air. He would choose to grace us with his appearance for five minutes over dinner (or not), and then go to bed and sleep until the next morning, when he would get up and do the same over again. Work hard, drink, sleep. His life was relegated to the basics in life. While I was reaching self-actualization on Maslow's hierarchy of needs, Michael was floundering at the basic physiologic level.

At times, however, that loud, thundering freight train ready to run me over with his biting verbal abuse would appear. With a quick barb thrown my way, he had a way of making me feel as small as an ant sitting atop Mount Everest. There was an occasional clock bulleted at the bedroom wall, or a tirade about not wearing an expensive piece of jewelry he'd bought me for some occasion. Sometimes he lost chunks of time, and I'd have to repeat conversations from as recently as a day before. Living with an active alcoholic is like being a Mexican jumping bean; it's physically and emotionally exhausting.

The healthier and more emotionally strong I became, the more I believe Michael felt threatened. I thrived, and his disdain for me became more evident with the passage of time. Michael was like a pot of boiling pasta, the bubbles getting ready to explode over the pot's side and scorch the pristine stovetop. Both Janelle and I tried to steer clear of the impending scalding froth.

Whatever his behavior, I loved Michael. I took my wedding vows seriously, and I meant "for better or worse, in sickness and in health." After all, he had stuck by my side during my insanity, and that could not have been an easy task for him either. I'm sure there were days he wanted to say "chuck it," or something that rhymes with the phrase, but he stuck by me, and I was going to stick by him.

Many people caught up in the family dynamics of alcoholism tend to look only at the behaviors of the alcoholic. They try to reason and use logic with the ill individual. You can't do either, because the ill person is beyond reason or logic. Their reality is in their own pickled head. At some point, without help from others, it's too difficult to deal with the alcoholic person and their behavior. People end up abandoning the relationship, or severing all ties to the alcoholic. I've seen it happen over and over again. If people could only understand this disease, it wouldn't be such a devastating malady for marriages and families. I believe the cure starts with education.

Since I was lucky enough to be an alcoholic myself, I tried to look at Michael and his behavior differently than most folks. I looked at him as an afflicted person, and I knew deep down he was disgusted with his own behavior and thus took his anger and disappointment in himself out on those closest to him. For some reason, his sister, Jane, and I historically were his verbal punching bags. So be it.

Before I was healthy, the instances of put-downs and verbal or emotional abuse would trigger my binge drinking. In my healthy state, I just let the invectives role off my back like water on ducks' feathers. The less reaction Michael got from me, the more frustrated he became. The more he drank, the angrier he would become, and the cycle would continue. It was Michael who was now on the Ferris wheel that wouldn't end. Luckily, I had gotten off along the way and was now enjoying the entire amusement park, while he was left spinning round and round, up and down.

One blustery winter morning, I went to the public library. I was perusing the section on alcoholism, looking for a specific piece of literature someone had mentioned worth reading. I came across a book that was called something like *Why Alcoholics Don't Quit Drinking*. That isn't the exact name, but it was something like that. There was something intriguing about the red and black spine and title that caught my attention, so I pulled it off the shelf. I glanced at the front of the book, and the author's picture imbedded within the stiff, glossy cover gazed right at me with a look of stubborn determination. He looked about sixty years old, had pale blue eyes, and a head of white, distinguished-looking hair. He looked polished and powerful. I was immediately drawn to the author, as he could have passed for my father's brother.

I glanced over the first page of the small-sized book and read the first paragraph. Something in those sentences must have sparked my interest. Before long, I found myself seated in an orange and brown plaid chair in front of the electric fireplace devouring the entire book.

Although there wasn't a lot of new information for me, I liked how the book presented the concepts through personal synopses of alcoholic men and women and the effects of the disease on the entire family system. Usually, the stories featured individuals who were extremely intelligent and successful. It also spoke of how the author intervened in helping people with addictions before it was too late.

The author went on to talk about his method of "intervention," and how he offered a one- on-one approach to intercede in the alcoholic's life, instead of the more usual full-frontal attack of an entire family intervention. This guy made a lot of sense to me. Finishing the last chapter, I turned to the back cover to find one simple statement: "For assistance or more information, contact me at: Brian#####@###. com." I went home and emailed "Brian" that day.

On the home front, I truly felt that the train was about to crash. It might take six months or a year, but I could "feel" things coming to a head. I didn't know if Michael would get a DUI, be killed in a car accident or fired from his job, or experience deteriorating health due to alcohol consumption. I didn't want Janelle to think it was normal to live in a dysfunctional household. A promise I made to myself when I entered treatment was I would do whatever it took to break this cycle of addiction in the next generation. Having completed the first step by getting healthy, I was ready to take the next step toward that goal—seeing Michael become healthy.

The day my email reached Brian, he emailed me back. We talked about Michael, some of my history, and where I was in the recovery process. He said he had never worked with anyone so knowledgeable about this disease process, and he felt that with our combined efforts, we could switch tracks on this train's course. Brian was in recovery himself, and we bonded over our shared ailment. It was a sense of relief for me to speak with someone both educated on the complex illness we were dealing with and successful in intervening in family situations such as ours. I told him if I hired him, I wanted an intervention done in the most private of ways, treating my husband with the respect and dignity he deserved. I was also adamant that Janelle would be kept out of any proceedings.

After our initial conversations, I asked him to send me a packet of information to review and any contract arrangement. He told me that due to the nature of his business, he didn't subscribe to contracts. There were so many variables in dealing with addiction that he made no promises of outcomes. His goal would be to get Michael to a treatment facility. Period.

I obtained the intervention information within two days. I also watched a clip of Brian speaking on CNN about addiction. I liked him. He was speaking my language. The first page of the eight-page proposal was a simple illustration: a ring buoy you would use to throw to a drowning victim at sea. He nailed that one. That is exactly how I felt. I needed a life preserver to save this family. Price tag on that ringed life preserver: $20,000.

Brian's company literature explained that after wiring an initial $10,000 to his account, which was his retainer fee, he would begin making plans for the intervention that would need to take place. Once he received the second $10,000, the intervention would take place within seventy-two hours.

It was February 2006, and not only did I feel as if the train was going to collide, but all the stars were in alignment. It was going to be our twentieth wedding anniversary. Michael was turning fifty that year. He was making a boat-load of money. We would be getting at least $20,000 back in taxes this year. The squirrel cage in my brain started rattling away.

Although with Michael's salary we were spending more money than we ever had in our lives, I was still quite frugal. I usually bought things that were on sale, and I didn't spend a lot of money on myself. We didn't go out to eat. I cleaned my own house. Never, ever, would I even consider making a $20,000 purchase of any kind without discussing it with Michael. We were both on the same page with regard to finances. Save and live within your means ... always!

I took about a week to mull things over. I discussed the plan with Brian. I talked over the issues taking shape with Geri and other trusted AA members who had longevity in the program. They felt I had weighed all variables and covered all possible scenarios on how this intervention might play out. I received their blessing.

The following month, we received our tax money back. I knew I had a short window of time before Michael would ask about the money, so I signed our names to the state and federal checks and deposited $25,000 in our joint checking account. Michael let me handle all finances, taxes, and bills, so I was used to handling matters revolving around household money matters.

I then went to the bank and wired $10,000 to Brian's account. I was standing in line at the bank, literally shaking and having a panic attack. I felt short of breath and like I was about to pass out. The wire went through without a hitch, and I felt like breaking down in tears. What had I done? I was putting my trust and a lot of money into a man I had never met who lived on the East Coast. Even though I was panicked over having spent a significant amount of money, I was more panicked about Michael's reaction once he found out what I had done. It was time to get this ball really moving in earnest.

nelly

Michael was going to be attending a conference in Milwaukee, WI. The plan was as follows: Brian was going to fly to Milwaukee and intercept Michael at the hotel. Part of Brian's process was to be armed with a letter from me—a loving letter asking Michael to please accept Brian's help and enter treatment. I had already called our insurance company and received approval for a stay at a highly recommended treatment facility in West Palm Beach, Florida that Brian had suggested. I had contacted the staff there, and they spoke very highly of Brian and the facility's track record with positive outcomes and treatment of executive level persons. All pieces of the puzzle were starting to fit together nicely.

Michael was going to be in Milwaukee on March 6th. On March 3, 2006, I went to the bank and repeated the wire of money to complete the $20,000 transaction. I'm surprised I didn't pee my pants. I once again was very scared of the repercussions for what I was doing, yet I knew I had already started down the path, so I needed to see it through.

There were only two people that knew what I was doing, other than my AA small group—my mother and Brian. Both encouraged me to follow through and said that I was doing the right thing. Yet I was petrified. I felt like I was betraying Michael, since I was covertly planning all this activity. I kept Janelle in my vision at all times, and I wanted this for me and a healthy marriage, but more so for her to have a healthy, present father in her life. He had missed so much already.

On March 5, I received a call from Brian. He was supposed to be flying into Milwaukee. He called to tell me he wasn't on a plane. He said he had met with his business associates, and they felt that surprising Michael at a work function in Milwaukee was not a good way to conduct the intervention.

My heart fell to my feet. *Shit, I've been scammed. I'm dead!*

CHAPTER 29

BRIAN

I came completely unglued. "What do you mean you aren't on a plane? I wired you all the money! The intervention is supposed to be within seventy-two hours!" I'm sure Brian felt the panicked timbre through the phone. "Do you have any idea what will happen to me once Michael finds out about the money?" I said in a shrill voice.

"Relax and calm down," Brian said on a very even keel.

He explained to me that he wasn't comfortable with the current plan. He wasn't sure how Michael would take the approach at a business function. Usually, the interventions were done in the home setting. Because of my insistence that Janelle be kept out of the picture, we had taken the approach of having the intervention done away from the home front. Now, after discussion with others, he wasn't comfortable with that strategy.

"Now what?" I said, on the verge of hyperventilating.

"Well, I don't feel it's reasonable to tackle Michael with this out of the blue. Are you sure you don't want to arrange an intervention with you and Janelle in the home?"

"No, I don't want her involved," I said with conviction in my voice. Silence ensued while both of us pondered the predicament.

"What about if you called Michael on the phone and spoke to him?" I said.

"Don't you think he'd be really confused or angry if he got a call from me unexpectedly?" asked Brian.

"I don't know what his reaction would be. My guess is he would be professional on the phone. It would be better than lambasting him out of left field. If he gets angry, he'll probably take it out on me after the phone conversation in a verbal confrontation. But I'm used to that. I just don't see any other way around this. Pretty soon he'll ask about our tax return money, and I will have to say something!"

On Friday, March 10, Michael had come home from work early. It was a nice sunny spring-like day with temperature in the mid-sixties.

"I just got done delivering flags to churches with Marcia," he said in a happy mood. "She left for her cottage, and I decided to come home early."

Marcia was a co-worker and part of the fraternal company they worked for, and Michael's best friend at work. They would occasionally give out free American flags to area businesses as a community benefit and goodwill gesture.

"Have we gotten our tax money back yet?" Michael asked nonchalantly as he searched the fridge looking for something to snack on.

"I was going to talk to you about that," I said sheepishly. "I was thinking once we get the tax return money, I could get you a surprise fiftieth birthday present. I know we usually use the money to pay down the mortgage, but I was thinking this year is special in terms of it being our twentieth anniversary and your big fiftieth. I'd like to get you something special."

I could hear myself talking ... bullshitting away ... while my insides were melting like butter over warm toast.

"Huh ... why not?" he said, reacting in a positive way I wouldn't even have thought possible.

I'm sure he was thinking that I'd buy him a sports car or something along those lines, as he talked about that occasionally. He had no idea what my plan was, and I thanked God silently for letting the lies from my lips flow forth so easily. I felt major conflict. The biggest part of the AA program revolves around the ability to be honest, and here I was lying to Michael. I felt like the biggest fraud on earth. This would have definitely been a trigger for my drinking in the past. I had to keep it together.

I talked to Brian, and he was very supportive and definitely understood my feelings of discord. Unfortunately, that was the nature of the beast we were fighting. The conspiracy needed to be kept under wraps at all costs! In my hours of ambivalence, I would hash things over with Brian, my mother, or Geri, and I was supported in the fact that it was the "right thing to do."

That night, Michael and I were in bed sleeping. At 10:30 p.m., the phone rang. We assumed it was our neighbor, who historically would call me late at night after getting a snoot full and want to talk on the phone for hours. I was going to let the phone ring, but for some reason Michael answered it, probably ready to tell the neighbor off for calling at such an hour.

"Hello," Michael said groggily, scooting to the edge of the bed, shoulders slumped.

A moment of silence passed. "You're kidding!" His shoulders and back snapped to attention at whatever news was imparted.

"Oh my God, that's terrible! I don't know what to say. How did it happen? Uh huh ... uh huh ... uh huh. I just can't believe it. Okay. Thanks. I'll talk to you tomorrow. Shit! Thanks ... okay ... goodbye." Michael hung up the phone.

"What happened?" I asked, thinking someone in the family was hurt, maybe Michael's brother.

"Marcia's dead! After I left her today, she drove to the cottage. Her car flipped. The police think she overcorrected the car for some reason. She was on a straight road, and the weather was nice, so they think maybe her phone dropped on the floor or something. She wasn't wearing a seat belt, which was unusual for her. She was thrown from the car and was killed instantly upon impact."

Not only had Michael just lost a really good friend, he'd lost a valued co-worker as well. He was pall bearer at her funeral, and the next several weeks were gloom and doom dealing with the passing of Marcia. Michael was remorseful, quiet, and drinking a lot. He looked bloated, sweaty, and miserable at her funeral. It was not a good time to spring an intervention, so we waited.

Sometime in April, Brian called Michael. Brian introduced himself to Michael and told him what he did for a living, and that he had been hired by me to assist with Michael's drinking problem. He relayed to me that Michael was very cordial on the phone and said, "I don't want to discuss that issue." End of story. Michael never told me about the conversation with Brian, and we never discussed the exchange.

A month or so later, Michael asked me about the tax return money. I told him I used the money to pay for Brian's services to help him with his drinking problem. Michael looked at me like I was an alien with two heads, but he never mentioned another word about it. I could tell the pot was quietly simmering, but it never boiled over, and he didn't mention the money again.

Brian would call Michael once a month or so for the next six months. Michael listened to what Brian said, but always ended the conversation with, "I'm not ready to discuss this." I stayed out of the situation, and there were no further discussions between Michael and me regarding the money or his drinking problem.

I was getting restless. Things were escalating on the home front. Anger bursts from Michael were accelerating. Janelle overheard me talking on the phone to Brian and wondered who Brian was. I explained I was asking for his help with Dad's drinking issue. She was fully aware of her dad's aberrant behavior, and I would explain that her dad was sick and I was trying to help him. She was nine years old but understood things that teenagers would have a difficult time understanding. I was always straightforward and truthful with Janelle.

If she asked, I would find an age appropriate way to respond to her questions honestly.

I told Brian that something had to give soon before something really bad happened to Michael. He agreed.

At the end of October, 2006, Michael was going to be near the East Coast in New York for a business function. I asked Brian if the intervention could happen in New York. He agreed to take the train from his Connecticut home to New York where Michael would be staying. Now that Michael knew who Brian was via phone calls, it wouldn't be such a surprise to have Brian show up at Michael's business function.

All was arranged. The intervention would finally happen. I was anxious, but felt relieved. Brian did travel to New York and called Michael from the hotel lobby where he was staying. Brian asked if Michael would come down from his room and meet with him. Michael refused and said once again, "I'm not ready to discuss this."

Brian traveled home without speaking to Michael in person. We got another bill for $600.00 traveling expenses for Brian. I was nearly at the end of my rope. It had been nearly nine months, and the baby wasn't being close to being delivered.

Then the bottom fell out.

CHAPTER 30

SUSIE

On Thursday, November 16, I was dressed in designer jeans and a shirt with a comfortable jean jacket, sitting at the airport terminal. I had reached my jogging goal of eight miles that morning, and the endorphins were still coursing through my bloodstream as I waited for Susie's plane to land.

Susie had decided to visit us for four days while John went deer hunting back in Wisconsin. I was excited to spend time with her, and Susie was looking forward to spending quality time with Janelle, her only niece.

I walked up the graduated plank way to greet Susie as she disembarked from the plane. I was all smiles and grabbed her in a big embrace. "So good to see you," I said delightedly.

"Well, you look young," she said flippantly, inspecting me from head to toe.

"I feel young ... but of course, I'm not the one turning fifty in a few months," I said in sassy retort.

Leaving the airport with my sister in tow, I asked if she wanted to stop by Michael's office, since it was on the way home and she had never seen where he worked.

"Sure, why not?" she replied casually.

Walking into the "Tower," as it was called, we pushed the elevator button for the nineteenth floor. I led the way to Michael's office, where he was sitting behind his expansive mahogany desk in his corner office overlooking the city's skyline. He was munching on a sandwich while staring at his computer screen when we walked in and surprised him. He hurriedly swallowed his lunch and got up to give us each a hug.

"Welcome to town," Michael said to my sister.

"Thanks. Nice digs you have here," my sister said, clearly impressed. "You've come a long way from where you started back at AAL." Susie had a slight edge to her voice. I'm sure Michael did not pick up on the negative inflection, but I did. I dismissed my sister's temperament as being tired from traveling all day. After chatting for a brief moment with Michael, I showed my sister around, and she met some of the big mucky- muck executives on Michael's floor. Then we drove home.

We spent Friday morning at the country club gym. We then went to Janelle's elementary school to have lunch with her. When you're in fourth grade, it's a big deal to have your mom spend lunch with you. It's even a bigger treat when your aunt accompanies her. We had a great time, and Susie met all of Janelle's little friends, her teacher and saw her school.

As we were driving through the Ridges, Susie admired the wealthy area we lived in. She thought the houses were beautiful and the area pretty. Living there, I took the scenery for granted, but it was a lovely area that had become our home.

We decided to take Janelle out of school and have a girls' shopping experience at Village Pointe, an upscale, outdoor shopping area five minutes away from where we lived. In another week, Michael was going to turn fifty, and Janelle and I were on the lookout for a birthday gift to give him. At one store, Susie picked up a box that contained a packet of paper the size of my grocery list. The pad was entitled "Scorecards." For some reason, Susie thought they were hilarious, and she wanted to give it to Michael as a gag gift. It had something to do with their common past performance management system when they both worked at AAL.

That evening, our family took Susie out for a nice dinner at Johnny's Steakhouse. As Michael and Susie began drinking pre-dinner cocktails, it felt like Janelle and I didn't exist. The two of them were talking back and forth and reminiscing like two long-lost friends. Michael evolved into prime form after a few cocktails and was verbally abusive toward me. Susie joined him in his onslaught of me: I wasn't fun because I didn't drink, and I was boring. And on it went. It got to the point where I had to excuse myself from the dinner table and go to the bathroom, tears brimming. I quickly composed myself so as not to arouse Janelle's suspicion. She was acutely perceptive when it came to me and my emotions. We got through the $200.00 dinner, me adding little in the way of conversation.

Saturday was a relaxing day. Susie, Janelle, and I went on a long walk around the golf course and explored the neighborhood. Janelle introduced Susie to her neighborhood friends, and she met my friends, which were the kids' mothers.

After the adoption process had fallen through a few years back, I had taken on the role of babysitting the neighbors' and my friends' infants. There were two I was especially close to, Westby and Owen. They were both under a year of age, and I would watch them when their moms had various appointments to go to. Our house would be the "drop off" house for babies. I got a lot of pleasure out of helping my friends, and I got my baby fix that way. Janelle loved having the infants around as well. It was as good a "sister" feeling as she would ever get. As we made our rounds, Susie was introduced to them all. It was another fun "girlie" day.

We got back to the house around 3:30 p.m. I began preparation for dinner, and Susie asked Michael if it was cocktail hour yet. Any hour of the day was cocktail hour for Michael, so of course he said yes. They went downstairs to the bar to mix up a couple of strong adult beverages as I was preparing dinner.

Janelle was putting some finishing touches on her Old North Church. It was a replica of the Boston Church related to Paul Revere's midnight ride during the Revolutionary War. She and Michael developed school projects together, and this one was a masterpiece. I helped Janelle with daily homework, and Michael was the man for occasional creative project work. Since his workshop contained two of every tool known to mankind, he was the go-to-guy for building artistry.

Michael and Susie were in the living room commingling over spirits when Susie decided to give Michael the gag gift she'd bought him. He opened the gift, and the two of them laughed their asses off. Janelle and I looked at each and shrugged our shoulders. Clearly, whatever humor the gift represented was lost on the two of us. Michael was almost doubled over he was laughing so hard. Susie was beside herself too.

I had grilled thick pork chops for dinner, knowing that was one of Susie's favorites. Couscous and fresh asparagus, along with homemade dinner rolls, finished the menu. I had made a choice chocolate dessert in Susie's honor as well. Halfway through dinner, Susie said, "This is really good. Where do you do your grocery shopping?"

"There is a Baker's down the road I go to, or I usually just stop at Super Target a few blocks away on my way home from the gym," I replied.

"I would never buy anything or serve our dog anything bought from Target," she said with an air of arrogance.

"Huh," I said, thinking to myself that I should mention there is Target food on her plate right now that she seems to be scarfing down okay.

Switching topics, I made the comment to Michael about how cute Owen looked when we went to visit his family today.

Susie interrupted, looking at me with disdain. "Oh, just be happy with what you have for God's sake!"

"I am happy with what I have. All I said was Owen looked cute today," I replied defensively, beginning to get perturbed by my sister's posture.

"Nelly just likes babies and likes to take care of them," Michael inserted, coming to my defense.

"I know you want another kid. You should just be thankful for what you have," Susie stated emphatically.

Michael and I exchanged a "what's up with her attitude" type of glance when Susie wasn't looking, and I just shook my head and got up to clear some dishes from the table to diffuse the situation.

During dinner, Susie commented that the meat "was too well done," the asparagus was "stringy," and the couscous was something Susie had "never eaten before" and wasn't sure if she liked its "texture or flavor." Really? Who made Susie Rachel Ray all of the sudden? Piss on her if she didn't like where I shopped or how I cooked. I kept my mouth shut.

After I cleaned up the kitchen, the three of us adults helped Janelle with her school project. Susie began to slur her words and make comments about the church décor. "This side looks like Ann Taylor Loft, and this side looks like Penny's," she proudly announced. What? Susie began making nonsensical statements, and Janelle looked at her aunt and said, "Auntie Susie, you're drunk!"

"I am?" Susie said with sheer surprise on her face. "I'll drink to that," and she took another gulp of what was now her third whiskey/Diet 7-Up. "I have to go to the bathroom. Where is it?" Janelle and I pointed her in the direction of the bathroom that she had already been to many times over the past few days.

While Susie was in the bathroom and Janelle was occupied, I pulled Michael aside.

"I am so sick of being around drunken assholes, and I'm not talking about you this time. Get her out of my sight. Take her downstairs and you can entertain her. I am done. I don't need any more crap coming from my sister. I get plenty of that from you!"

He knew I was mad and at my limit. When Susie came out of the bathroom, I said, "Janelle and I are going to make brownies for tomorrow. Why don't you and Michael go downstairs and talk."

"Okay," she said happily, oblivious to my agitation. She toddled down the stairs to the finished basement, Michael following dutifully behind … happy to leave his scolding, irate wife in the dust.

Then I called my mother to complain about Susie.

"I'm so sick of being around drunken assholes," I told Georgia.

"Well, I'm sorry that's happening. Just get her to bed to sleep it off," was Mom's retort.

If only I had been able to follow my mother's advice!

CHAPTER 31
THE END

Janelle and I made brownies. The smell of chocolatey goodness permeated the air. Quality time spent with my daughter put me in a better mood. After pulling the baked goods out of the oven, we decided to play a number of board games to finish off the night before Janelle's bedtime.

I could hear occasional snorts of male and female laughter filtering up through heat ducts and grated registers. I was busy entertaining a nine-year-old and knew my irksome sister was being entertained by Michael, so all was good in the house once again. Janelle was very curious about Susie's behavior. She really hadn't been exposed to a drunken person before. I know that sounds crazy with two alcoholics in the house, but neither of us had ever been or acted "drunk." Having her aunt act crazy had her young mind piqued.

Janelle would occasionally run downstairs to get a game out of the toy closet and come back up to report to me what was going on. At points during the evening hours, Janelle propped herself on the top step leading down into the basement so she could eavesdrop. The reports from child to mother kept coming:

"Aunt Susie just made another drink ... I tried to stop her, but she wouldn't listen ... Auntie Susie just got mad at me and told me I should go play by myself and leave the adults alone ... Am I too much of a girlie girl? Aunt Susie told me I was, and she doesn't like girlie girls ... Is Auntie Susie really going to leave Uncle John? I think they're talking about sex ... Auntie Susie just told dad she's going back to her high school boyfriend. What does that mean?" And on it went. I tried to explain to Janelle that Auntie Susie was drunk and was saying stupid stuff, and tomorrow she'd wake up feeling bad and be sorry for her behavior.

"She will apologize for hurting your feelings," I said, trying to soothe Janelle's ruffled pride.

After getting Janelle off to bed around 9:00 p.m., I decided I'd better join my inebriated sister and render aid to Michael if he needed reinforcement. As I came down the stairs, I saw Michael stretched out and looking relaxed on one end of an elongated half U-shaped couch. His hands were linked behind his head, feet propped up on the table in front of him. Susie was sitting a body length away on the same couch within reach of the round glass coffee table. Her feet were tucked neatly under her ample buttock. As I entered the room, the conversation stopped.

A fragrant candle placed mid-table had flickering flames that danced off the basement walls. There were two full cocktails on the table. Susie's drink was the color of light molasses with a few ice cubes bobbing about. Michael's drink appeared to have been sitting there awhile. It looked diluted with no traces of ice left. Michael began his day drinking on the weekends, so my guess was he had stopped consuming alcohol hours ago. He was usually in bed by this time, snoring away.

Susie spotted me. "Well, it's about time you joined us," she said as she reached for her drink.

"I was busy taking care of a child," I said, derision lining my retort. I took a seat at the far end of the couch, away from both of them. The couch had a natural chaise lounge built into it, so I plopped down in recumbent position and sighed in relief, as if putting a period on the end of a long sentence.

I had no more than sat down when I looked at my sister and saw her eyes rolling back in her head as her head swayed back and forth. Looking at her, I felt like I was in a bad "Chucky" movie. "How much has she had to drink?" I asked Michael.

He shrugged his shoulders. "I wasn't keeping track."

Susie's eyes snapped back in place, and she repeatedly slurred "Nelly" as she pointed with her head first toward me and then toward Michael.

"What?" I said, my earlier irritation abruptly taking hold again.

"You know," Susie said.

"I don't have any idea what you're trying to say," I said rather disgustingly.

"How long has it been since you guys had sex?" she asked.

"Don't go there, Susie," Michael forcefully interrupted.

"Oh, okay. Why don't you lie down and let Nelly rub your feet?" Susie instructed Michael.

My "uncomfortable meter" began its ascent. *What the hell have these idiots been discussing down here?*

Michael jumped on Susie's suggestion. Lying down with his head near where Susie was sitting, he stuck his feet on my abdomen, indicating it was time for them to be rubbed. Susie, as if on cue, shifted down to where Michael's head rested and placed his head on her lap, beginning to stroke his hair. My "uncomfortable meter" took off like a Roman candle on the fourth of July.

"What the hell are you doing Susie?" I demanded.

"If you don't jump his bones, then I will," she declared, eyes rolling around like wheels on a moving car.

I threw Michael's feet to the side and jumped up off the couch. I started leaving the room. "You have to be fucking kidding me," I said.

"You two want to screw each other, be my guest. I am done with both of you and all this shit!"

Susie piped up and asked innocently, "Nelly, what's wrong? Where are you going?"

"You just said you wanted to jump my husband's bones. Where do you think I'm going? You two are disgusting. Have at 'er; you have my blessing!" This was the absolute last straw for me.

I was so angry as I reached the main floor, I was seeing red. *Am I the only fucking sane person in this house?* I collapsed on the living room chair, suddenly exhausted from the culmination of the past nine months. I didn't know what else to do, so I turned the television on to watch the news and calm myself down with some semblance of normality.

A minute later, my sister came bolting up from downstairs and slumped on the couch across from me, her eyes no longer rolling back in her head but moving to and fro from me to the television and back again. I silently seethed as I watched her bizarre mannerisms. Michael came up from downstairs and drifted into the kitchen to get a glass of water.

After a few seconds of playing volleyball with her eyes, Susie whispered, "Keep him away from me!"

"Keep who away from you?" I asked in an infuriated manner.

"Him," she said as she nodded her head toward Michael, who was by the sink in the kitchen.

"Oh, for God's sake, you're fine," I said. I was transported back to my sister's paranoia I observed before her psychiatric hospitalization. *Crap, she acted like this before. She's going to end up in the hospital again. John is going to kill me!*

At that point, Michael came into the living room and sat on the loveseat across the room from both my sister and me. All three of us stared at the TV like we were suddenly captivated by the weather report. Michael abruptly rose from the loveseat, spread a nearby throw on the floor, and proceeded to lie down on the blanket. "Why don't we all watch a movie," he suggested.

Michael had the TV remote in hand and changed the station. My senses were instantly assaulted in that darkened living room. On the screen, larger than life, was a gorgeous, dark-haired, exotic looking woman in the arms of a muscled young man. They were naked and groaning. Dark skin and light skin intertwined in a passionate embrace.

"Oh my God," I said, "you're disgusting!" Before the titillating scene progressed further, I once again got up and left the living room to climb upstairs to our bedroom. I felt like I needed to keep escaping depravity in my own house. I left Michael sprawled on the floor, watching his lewd television broadcast.

Again, like a little puppy, my sister followed me up the stairs. As I was pulling down the covers to my bed, she faltered in the entryway of my room and declared in a slurred manner, "Well, I am certainly not used to this!"

I stopped cold. I wheeled around to face my sister in the doorway, hands fisted on both hips. I was completely incensed. "And you think this is how I live? You two are absolutely nuts. You do what you want. I am going to bed!" Like a deflating balloon, I took a deep breath and let out the air in my lungs. I was emotionally spent from the night's activity, and said in a kinder, softer tone, "You're drunk, Susie. Just go to bed. *Please!*"

"Okay." Off my sister toddled like a small child relegated to her room.

About ten minutes later, Michael came into our room. He crawled into bed and reached for me in his aroused state. It was obvious to me his amorous switch was turned on and he was still trying to get lucky. I lay there like a plank, non-responsive to his caresses. All at once, Michael threw back the bed covers. "I'm going to go get your sister to join us," he said.

I rocketed out of bed like the mattress was on fire and raced into the hallway. Michael was already at my sister's bedroom door. "No you're not," I shouted. "You leave her alone!" I was outraged and sickened. I found myself positioned half-way down the staircase, looking up the banister toward Michael, who was teetering and trying to steady himself in the door frame to Susie's bedroom.

I felt dazed and was frozen mid-step. I heard Michael mumble something to Susie. From inside her room, I heard my sister respond to him. Her response was short, and I heard her mention my name. That was all I heard. I was still seeing red, and my body was on fire. Every nerve ending was on heightened alert, and I was yelling at Michael once again to leave my sister alone.

"It [his desired threesome] isn't going to happen," he said, turning toward me.

I looked at him and screamed. "Of course it isn't. Are you fucking out of your mind?"

I will never forget the look on his face. He looked right at me and said very seriously and calmly, "Yes … I think I am." With that response, he meandered toward our bedroom and crawled into bed.

With the crisis de-escalated and my sister and husband safely tucked into their respective beds, I crumbled on the stairs in a heap and began sobbing.

I cried.

And cried.

And cried some more.

Sometime later, devoid of further emotions, I sat down in the computer room near the base of the stairs and did two things. I emailed Brian and said "it" had happened. The bottom had fallen out. I told him I could no longer handle my life the way it was. Something had to happen, and I needed it to happen *now!*

Secondly, I started journaling. I pounded the keyboard. All my feelings, everything that had happened that night and over the past nine months' teeter totter of emotions, came raining down and splashed across the computer screen.

nelly

It felt as though I had traveled to another dimension that night, and I was living in the Twilight Zone. I could actually hear the "*do do do do..do do do do*" anthem of the popular TV show of the early 1960s. I half expected Rod Serling or Alfred Hitchcock to materialize any moment. I was mesmerized by the computer screen with the cursor blinking back at me and the soft glow of Janelle's blue lava lamp perched next to me on the small desk.

But Rod and Alfred never materialized. All was quiet in the house the remainder of the night. Everyone was anchored in their respective bedrooms. I monitored both my husband's and sister's snoring patterns, making sure they remained safely passed out in their debauched slumber. I remained tiredly attentive until 3:00 a.m., when every ounce of my being was depleted. I finally leaned back in the desk chair, eyeballing the lava lamp and feeling much like the weightless blob of yellow goop flowing up and down its vertical path.

The next day, despite feeling numb when Michael came downstairs, I began the verbal smack down.

"You are one sick bastard," I said to Michael as I busied myself making coffee.

"What are you talking about?" Michael said with a pissed-off attitude.

"Well, let's try wanting to have sex with my sister and me last night for one thing." I couldn't even look at the man I'd married.

After a pregnant pause, he responded like a two-year-old responding to his parent after a sibling fight: "She started the whole thing," he said defensively.

"I don't care if the fucking dogs started it. You are responsible for your behavior, and I am so tired of you and your drinking. I am done, Michael. If you don't get help, there is nothing left here," I said, wildly waving my arms back and forth from him to me, as if trying to emphasize my words.

Michael vaguely remembered parts of the previous evening. He remembered me coming downstairs after putting Janelle to bed. He remembered Susie saying she wanted to jump his bones, but he didn't remember anything after that. Not the blanket on the floor, or the erotic TV show, or suggesting that the three of us have sex. How convenient ... although the way our conversation went, I actually believed him.

My sister came down the stairs still dressed in the brown corduroys and sweater she'd passed out in the night before. I was still busying myself in the kitchen.

Susie came bounding toward me. "What happened last night?" she asked, panic lining her voice.

I rotated slowly from the sink to come face to face with her. "You ... don't know ... what happened last night?" I asked emphatically.

"No, I just remember running up the stairs from downstairs. That was right after dinner, wasn't it?" she said, confusion plastered over her face.

"No, you came upstairs about 10:15 last night," I said cautiously. "What exactly do you remember?"

"I don't remember anything after dinner," she said.

"Nothing?" I began my tirade. "You don't remember being a jerk to me at dinner? Hurting Janelle's feelings? You don't remember saying you wanted to jump Michael's bones? You don't remember saying you were going to leave your husband for your high school boyfriend? None of that?"

As each sentence came out of my mouth, it looked like my sister was getting closer to throwing up.

"No, I don't remember anything other than sitting down to dinner," she said, obviously trying hard to remember and feeling panicked that she couldn't.

I can't explain what happened next, except that it was like a light switch clicking on for me. Every strange occurrence from my sister's past was at the forefront of my brain—her psych hospitalization, losing a job she wouldn't discuss, her anxiety attacks, and other events.

It struck me like a bolt of lightning: *You are one of us—an alcoholic.* With that sudden realization, my demeanor softened toward my sister.

"Is this your first blackout?" I asked gently.

"Yes," she replied without pause. Her response was too quick.

Yeah, right, I thought to myself.

I proceeded to tell my sister the deranged happenings of the previous night. By the end of my report, she looked sickly and sallow. "Oh my God," she said. "What am I going to tell John?" She spoke more to herself than to me.

"The truth! That's all you can do. He'll understand," I assured her.

The milieu for the rest of the day was rather morose. Michael licked his wounds and stayed sheepishly ensconced in our bedroom, only coming out for necessities such as nourishment. He knew I was furious.

The conversations with my sister revolved around why her deviant behavior had occurred the previous night. We discussed our genetics and predisposition to the disease of alcoholism. I shared with her what treatment was like, and encouraged her to go home and seek help. My sister was so ashamed and horrified by how she'd acted that she seemed absolutely open to getting aid when she returned home.

As I discovered later that day while tidying up the basement, my sister and husband had gone through a full two-liter bottle of whiskey. According to Michael, he had made only three drinks the previous evening, and his third drink remained untouched on the table. That meant my sister had consumed three quarters of the bottle herself in a short span of time, about eight hours.

I'm surprised we didn't end up taking Susie to the hospital to get her stomach pumped. She could have died by vomiting and aspirating if she'd puked in her sleep the night before. That day, I realized how serious things could have gotten. Even though the prior evening had been awful for me personally, it could have really turned into a nightmare had I not been there monitoring the situation. After discovering how much alcohol had been consumed, it was no wonder my sister had been in a six-hour blackout.

As the day progressed into nightfall, my shock over the twisted behavior waned, and my concern over what could have happened slowly ebbed. I silently thanked God that nothing really bad had happened. Yet.

CHAPTER 32

HELP!

Susie left on Monday, November 20, in the early morning hours. She decided to take a taxi to the airport instead of riding with Michael and being dropped off at the Delta terminal on his way to work. The atmosphere in the house had been tense, but tolerable, the day before. The girls hung out, Susie was sullen, and Michael kept to himself. The four of us co-mingled only at dinner.

As my sister was getting into the cab, I said, "Now go home and get some help!" I hugged my sister hard, trying to transfer my strength and encouragement to her, because I knew what difficult steps were in front of her in dealing with her alcoholism.

"Don't worry. I'll have no trouble doing that," she said somewhat flippantly, yet convincingly.

After sending my sister off, I spent the rest of the day putting the house in order and making plans for the upcoming hectic week. I touched base via phone with Brian for an update on Michael, but didn't have time to go into details or make definitive plans due to the Thanksgiving holiday week ahead. We decided to talk again early the following week.

On Tuesday, I took Janelle out of school, as we had a pre-planned surprise fiftieth party for Michael with all his business associates at work. His assistant and I had collaborated to give him a surprise party. Janelle found it fun to have a goofy cake decorated in black, along with over the hill gag gifts. Michael's co-workers filtered in and out of the commons area, congratulating him and conversing with Janelle and me. Michael was quite surprised by the unsolicited attention, and I played the proud, dutiful wife. Georgia would have been proud!

On Wednesday, Michael's best friend from college, Dave, was driving down from Minnesota, as was Michael's sister, to surprise him again for his birthday as well as join us for Thanksgiving. I was busy cleaning and getting dinner preparations under way.

Both Dave and Jane showed up Wednesday afternoon and surprised Michael. He was happy they had made the effort to come and would be joining us for Thanksgiving. Dave walked in carrying a huge bottle of Grey Goose vodka and expensive cigars. Great!

The climate around Michael and me remained tense, and when Dave and Jane asked what was up, I replied, "Michael got pretty drunk the other night."

"Yeah," he said, "things got a little out of hand."

Both Jane and Dave could tell it was a tender subject and let it drop. Nothing more was said.

Thanksgiving dinner turned out well, and we all had fun, despite the strained atmosphere. Later that day, we called Grandma Georgia to wish her a happy Thanksgiving.

"Hi, Mom, happy Thanksgiving."

"I wish it were," she replied snappishly.

"What do you mean?" I asked.

"Well, Susie and John just left, and all I can say is you better get your husband some serious help," she said curtly.

"Well, what do you think I've been trying to do for the last eight months?" I said carefully. "Why?"

"Susie told us what happened at your house, and all I can say is get your husband help. Now!" Georgia barked out.

"Hold on. What are you talking about? How is Susie? Is she acting okay?"

"She's acting fine, but I have to go now," Georgia said in a contemptible manner. "Just do what I said and get Michael some help!"

I got off the phone and was extremely confused. My mother's response was her usual cryptic and dramatic jargon, but I really didn't have time to analyze the exchange with holiday guests in the house. My concern was for the welfare of my sister and how she was doing psychologically. I wondered if she had taken any steps in getting assistance for her illness. I was glad to hear she was acting normally, however, and my fears that she was a resident in a psychiatric facility again weren't realized.

On Friday, November 24, 2006, Michael's sister left to drive home. Dave and Michael were out shooting games of pool before Dave traveled home to Minneapolis later that day.

At 1:30 p.m., Susie called. Seeing it was my sister's number on caller ID, I answered cheerfully. "Hello."

"I just want to let you know what I've done since leaving your house," Susie said rather matter-of-factly.

Super she's going to tell me she has taken steps to get help liked we discussed. "Sure, what's up?" I asked casually.

"Well, first of all I need to apologize for being snotty at your house. John tells me I get that way when I drink once in a while."

She was a hell of a lot more than "snotty," but whatever. "That's an understatement," I said benevolently.

"Nelly, we just got back from a local rape crisis center, and I've been tested for STDs, AIDS, and pregnancy. I also had a pelvic exam," continued my sister in a monotone fashion, like she was reading a script.

"What ... what ... what on earth are you talking about?" I asked, thinking this was a joke and she'd break out in laughter soon.

John piped in from another phone line, shouting angrily. "You don't know what hell you have just put us through!"

"Wait a minute," I said protectively. "What we ... have put ... you ... through?" I emphasized every word carefully. "Susie, you drank three-quarters of a bottle of whiskey that night. You put Michael's head on your lap, you were rubbing his hair, and then you were the one wanting to jump his bones. You were in a six-hour blackout, for God's sake. Are you frickin' kidding me?"

Click went the extension John was on.

"I just wanted you to know what steps we've taken since I got home. I thought you'd want to know. We sat down before Thanksgiving dinner yesterday and discussed it with Mom and Dallas. They said I should call and let you know," Susie said with a flat affect. "That's all."

Another *click* and then the steady tone of a dead line. Cue in the "do do do do ... do do do do" music of *The Twilight Zone.*

Somehow during the brief dialogue, I was transported from inside my house to the back deck. I must have done so automatically so that Janelle wouldn't pick up on my rising angst. I stood on our deck with a beautiful landscape before me. Multi-million dollar houses off in the distance, a manicured rolling golf course, neighborhood kids' squeals of delight playing childhood games in the vicinity ... and all I could do was stare at a phone receiver in disbelief as the muffled dial tone gave evidence of an unfathomable conversation. My life as I knew it dissolved before my eyes, and my heart flat lined like the dial tone.

Waking out of my fugue state, I heard the door leading into the house from the garage slam shut. I ran through the kitchen and up to Michael and Dave as they were jawing back and forth about shots taken in the pool hall and who owed who money for the side bets of ace shots.

Michael must have seen the look of sheer terror on my face, as he stopped cold mid-stride. Everything came tumbling out of my mouth all at once. I didn't care that Dave was witness to my hysterics or not. My anxiety was palpable.

nelly

"My sister just called, and she said she was at a rape center and had all these tests done. She thinks she was raped by you! Oh my God … what the hell are we going to do? She's crazy… John was on the phone and was yelling at *me* about the hell *we* put *them* through. He hung up on me before I could even explain what had happened … Susie sounded weird, like totally disconnected … they sat down yesterday before Thanksgiving dinner with my mom. They must have told them she was raped … I can't believe it … Oh my God …Oh my God …"

The mood changed from celebratory to depressed instantly. Michael led the way as the three of us lumbered into the living room. Wordlessly, we collapsed on nearby furniture, trying to digest what had been alleged. We were in a state of shock. Michael stared at the carpeted floor and gently shook his head back and forth. I'm sure he saw his future dissipate as well. Dave was a lawyer and had stood up in our wedding with my sister, so he knew the players involved. Dave was a large presence. He was verbose and fun-loving in nature, but his garrulousness was now mute. There was really nothing any of us could say. The accusation was so revolting; my stomach contents were about ready to be purged on that same carpeted floor.

Dave left. Michael quit drinking alcohol cold turkey. On his actual fiftieth birthday he spent the day detoxing from alcohol. I knew quitting drinking on the spot was dangerous in a medical sense, so I was watchful. As we decorated the house for Christmas, Janelle wondered why her dad's hands were as shaky as a baby's rattle.

I called Brian. Michael sought counsel from a lawyer, who felt that the rape allegations would disappear. His advice was to do absolutely nothing with regard to my sister.

I told Michael he needed to seek treatment, whether or not he had quit drinking. I asked him to talk to Brian. He did. Brian convinced Michael to enter treatment. He privately asked for a month off from work, and it was granted. I took him to the airport. He flew to West Palm Beach, Florida and entered the Hanley Center for inpatient treatment.

I wasn't allowed to talk to Michael the entire time he was gone. His counselors kept in touch with me and said after the first week that Michael was doing "awesome." His treatment was three weeks long, and he decided to leave Florida in time to be home for Christmas Eve. Michael had been so absent from the home that no one in the neighborhood even knew he was gone for almost a month. Not one person, except Janelle and I, had even missed him.

The man that came through the door that Christmas Eve had changed. The constant anger simmering below the surface was no more. Instead of wanting more and more material wealth, he was full of gratitude for what we had. He stopped isolating himself and re-engaged in life. He was vulnerable, open, kind, and loving toward Janelle and me. Although he had to figure out what to do with all his free time, he was whole again. Janelle and I were happy to have a husband and father back. It was like we had awakened from a long winter slumber, and light was shining once again. Everything was green and spring-like in our home; seedlings of hope and forgiveness had been planted and were growing.

Within six months, his dad died unexpectedly and he lost his job.

CHAPTER 33

AFTER

The wonderful thing about being healthy and holding the Glinda's at bay is that you learn to cope with life on life's terms. The curve balls continue to come at you full force, yet you are able to adjust your catcher's mitt and lean left or right to pluck the ball mid-air. With the projectile safely ensconced in glove, you then center yourself securely behind home base and get on with the game of life.

Instead of being paralyzed by life, or just going through the motions, there is a sense of freedom and confidence that all you have to do is the "next right thing" and everything will work out. You learn to "let go and let God." There is no room for anger, resentments, fear, or loneliness. All the negative emotions are replaced with a sense of joy. Recovery is a miracle, and everyone that survives this devastating illness and remains active in a recovery program is in wonder of its power.

Michael, Janelle, and I continued to navigate the ups and downs of life and thrive.

Shortly after the allegations made by my sister, I went to see a psychologist that specialized in mental illness and recovery. He was also a long-standing AA member. I needed to have a conversation with someone objective who could help me wrap my mind around the insanity of my sister's behavior in the context of our diseased family.

Dr. Atherton, a soft-spoken, rounded, grandfatherly figure, ushered me into his simply furnished office. I told him my entire sordid story.

"Obviously, I can't diagnose your sister without doing a comprehensive assessment," he said. "But her behavior toward Michael, stemming back to when they worked together, makes me wonder if your sister isn't suffering from a personality disorder as well as alcoholism. I would suggest you continue to encourage her to get help. You'll have to figure out what type of relationship, if any, you want to maintain with her."

Over the next few months, I continued to encourage John to get my sister in for a formal psychological and/or alcohol assessment. John must have decided to do just that. In February of 2007, my sister phoned me and the conversation went like this:

"Hi, Nelly. I just wanted you to know that I had an alcohol assessment like you suggested. AA is not for me, so I decided to handle my alcoholism the way I want to. By the way, next weekend we're getting together for a picnic at the cottage with Mom and Dallas and were wondering if you, Michael, and Janelle would like to come and join us?"

Yeah, sure. After being accused of a violent felony by you and John, we would love to get together! It would be one big, happy family ... not to mention a comfortable occasion!

"Susie, I wish you all the luck in the world, but until you take steps to get healthy, I don't see how we can ever get together. You and John did a lot of damage to our family—all three of us. You hurt my child. You tried to destroy our marriage and family. Michael is more than willing to apologize for the part he had on that November night, but not until you're healthy enough to acknowledge your part. Until things are made right and you get yourself some concentrated help, we can't possibly get together. Good luck to you!"

This time I got to go *click*.

Nelly

I haven't talked to my sister since 2007.

Georgia decided to insert herself into the middle of the messy sisterly dynamics. According to Georgia, I am unforgiving, and my inability to absolve my sister has led to my mother's physical and mental decline. I have been accused of causing my mother's depression and heart disease, and I am the cause of the continued dysfunction in our family. I have literally been accused of killing my mother.

My mother has found it easier not to talk to any of us—her daughter, her only biological granddaughter, and Michael. She and Dallas won't step foot in our home.

Of course, Georgia continues to make excuses for Susie's behavior, and will proceed to allow my sister to get away with unstable behavior. Unfortunately, the enabling will continue until both are in their graves.

I have offered to help either my sister or mother any way I can with the illness they both have exhibited. I have offered to take a lie detector test or talk with any counselor they have seen.

My offers continue to go unacknowledged.

They are ill.

I understand.

CHAPTER 34

HAPPY ENDING

Life is one big circle, and as such we were now living back in Wisconsin. I was dressed in a pair of black slacks, a power red blazer, and newly polished black shoes. I looked and felt like a million bucks. It had been a number of years since I had worked outside the home. The interview with the largest health care provider in the area went well. I was offered the job and accepted.

One of my soon-to-be co-workers was escorting me out of the state-of the-art building as we said our parting remarks. As I was opening the door to leave, I heard a male voice from nearby holler, "Nelly?" A remote memory clicked at the sound of the voice, and as I turned toward the greeting I exclaimed, "Oh my God ... *Dan?*"

It had been thirty plus years since I'd seen this man and although time had marched on and he looked a little greyer and a little rounder, I recognized him instantly.

I sprinted toward him with a broad smile, and we embraced enthusiastically.

"It is so good to see you again," I said pleasantly. "I didn't know you lived here. How on earth have you been?"

"Really good, I didn't know you lived here either! What are you doing here?" he asked, sounding genuinely happy to see me.

The thirty plus years evaporated. We decided to sit down and chat in the entryway seating area and get caught up on each other's lives. Dan was president of a local bank and was visiting the health care facility because it was one of the bank's major accounts. He was married with three kids, all grown.

We reminisced about old times and people we had known, and updated each other on our current existence. After a fast and spirited hour, I said goodbye.

"I need to go now, I have to get home before Janelle gets home from school," I said somewhat regretfully. "It was so good to see you again. Take care of yourself!"

As Dan jumped to a stance, he reached to give me a hug goodbye "It was great to see you again too. You look so good and sound so happy!"

I slowly backed away from the entanglement. I looked into his eyes, and although I wanted to blurt out, "You'll never know the bullet you dodged by not ending up with me," I simply said, "I am happy. Really happy!"

Dan would never know how much it took for me to utter those ordinary words, much less to truly feel that way.

EPILOGUE

February 3, 2016

It was the third night sleeping in our living room in the ultra-comfortable recliner I had given Michael as a gift for Christmas a short time ago. The oxygen machine beside me provided white noise to Michael's sonorous slumber. The rhythmic bubbling of the distilled water was comforting as I drifted in and out of a light sleep.

At 2:00 a.m., I awoke to Michael's unconscious cry of presumptive discomfort. Perhaps his pain was caused from the pressure of the brain tumors themselves, or perhaps from the dying process. I didn't know. I gave him another shot of morphine and repositioned him in his hospital bed in our living room. I checked his vital signs and noticed his pulse had become noticeably weaker and thready in nature.

I woke Janelle, who was on leave from college due to her father's condition. She was now home from nursing school for the duration. She assisted me in providing her dad comfort. She lifted his head, and I flipped his pillow. It was feverish to the touch and filled with perspiration. She gave his mouth a rinse with oral swabs we had been given from Hospice. He had been sucking on them reflexively for moisture, but now his mouth lay agape. We changed his adult diaper due to soiling. I told Janelle I didn't think he would make it much longer.

nelly

Sixteen months ago, Michael, age fifty-eight, was diagnosed with brain cancer—the same thing that Harry had been diagnosed with many years ago. It was ultimately a death sentence, but Michael fought his "Glinda" valiantly over the past months.

Janelle and I tried to get more sleep but finally gave up at 5:00 a.m. At 7:00 a.m., his respirations were markedly abnormal with what we call Cheyne Stoking, or long periods of not breathing called apnea. Janelle was holding Michael's right hand, tears streaming down her face. She was mute except for the occasional hiccup from crying too hard and long.

I crawled into the hospital bed on Michael's left side ... the side closest to his heart I had occupied for thirty-six years. I linked my arm with his and told him I loved him and it was okay to go ... Janelle and I would be okay. Tears formed in a pocket beneath me, bouncing off Michael's arm. I told him I would miss him, and I do. He left us at 7:24 a.m. Before they took his body away for good, I kissed his cold forehead. Little did I know until later that Michael was standing behind me in angelic observation.

His ashes are in a gold container in our bedroom. I keep him close to me and talk to him daily. Beside his urn is a framed poem I had written to him in 1980. Although not grammatically correct, you will get the drift.

What I wish for is to be with you now
As I always do.
Because you are like I; and are a part of me.

I would like to begin each day
Only to awaken beside you,
And kiss you gently in morning greeting
While the sun's ray's play upon your stilled outline.

And share the subtleties of each day,
Whether it be to watch a simple sunset,

Or a child at play.
To receive each moments pleasure as one.

When distance separates us; my desire is to be near you.
And feel the contentedness once again
I experience in your mere presence.
The tranquility in my heart then, cannot be surpassed.

Our lives have intermingled; your happiness is mine.
When you hurt, I hurt more.
When you laugh, I laugh louder.
When you are lonely, I am indeed lonelier.

What I wish for is to be with you now
As I always do.
Because you are like I; and are a part of me.

I said early in the book that I am not afraid of death. I've seen much of it. When my last breath comes in this earthly world, my joy is knowing Michael will greet me with his beautiful smile. He will take my hand and we can continue our sweet love throughout eternity.

Today, however, Terry is divorced and lives in a town five miles from our cottage. Dan is now divorced and living in the same city as me, and Steve is single and contemplating moving back to Wisconsin. I've been in touch with each of them via Facebook thanks to Mark Zuckerberg! Who knows what the future may bring, but so far it has been one hell of a ride!

Anonymously,

Nelly

Coming Soon
Michael

CHAPTER 1
OCTOBER 27, 2014

I had a grave premonition. I was restless and anxious. Something... *or someone* was pushing me to get up early to start my day. At four a.m. the house was dark and still. I quietly brewed dark roast coffee in the Keurig, added a splash of hazelnut-flavored cream. Dressed in silk pajamas with a fragrant mug of steaming java warming both my hands, I shuffled to the cave-like bedroom on the main floor which housed my office. I logged on to my work computer.

After a few scalding sips of what I refer to as Norwegian gasoline, senses came alive. I became immersed in case files. I was heavily focused on two adjacent computer monitors atop my desk, beacons of light spewing forth patients' clinical information. I abstracted a variety of patient care information from an electronic medical record. I then uploaded the data to a contracted vendor who transmitted information to Medicare. My employer, a large hospital system, would get reimbursed for episodes of care partially based upon how well we were providing and documenting quality patient care according to industry standards. It wasn't a stimulating vocation for a nurse who used to physically take care of patients, but having this type of administrative work allowed schedule flexibility and the ability to work from home.

Michael

At age fifty-five, it was a perfect employment situation for the last phase of work life. Michael, now age fifty-eight and a Vice President of Sales and Marketing for an insurance company, was counting down the years to an early retirement.

Janelle was in her senior year of high school and had recently been accepted to a small, private college that specialized in her chosen field of study; Nursing, *A chip off the old block!* Once Janelle made it through college, Michael and I could afford to do anything we wanted in our golden years. We had our nest egg safely tucked away and both of us had been clean and sober for years. After many chaotic years, life was on an even keel. In recent months we discussed retirement living as snow birds. We would live at our cottage during the summer months and go south during the winter. At 6 a.m. all thoughts of the future came to a screeching halt!

"*MOM*, come down here...*FAST!*" Janelle screamed from the lower level of the home. Sheer panic was evident in her plea.

"Coming," I shouted back. I popped out of my desk chair like a Jack-In-The-Box toy upon final turn of the handle.

I sprinted down the staircase to the finished basement. Directly ahead I saw Michael bent over the back of our sectional couch. Plumber's crack greeted me in the early hour. There was a blue towel draped loosely around his waist, barely covering the essentials. Janelle, dressed in her wrinkled teenage sleeping attire and hair disheveled, was to the right of her father. Feet firmly planted in a Kung Fu stance, her left arm was wrapped tightly around his waist. With her right hand, she was desperately trying to keep her father from toppling over and keep his private parts covered... *with little success.*

"What on earth...?" I questioned.

"Get... me... to... the... couch," Michael grinded out with clenched teeth. He was shaking uncontrollably. His limbs looked like our anxious Jack Russell Terrier's quivering appendages.

I ran to the other side of Michael's six foot, one-hundred eighty pound frame. With Janelle and me flanking him, we lifted Michael around the back of the couch to the front, getting him in a prone position on the sofa cushions. Pure adrenaline surged through our bodies allowing such a feat. Michael was unable to assist.

Once he was settled into a semi-comfortable position, I perched myself on the edge of the couch and looked into Michael's blue eyes. I saw an expression I had never seen in the thirty plus years I had known him. It was a combination of terror, pain and panic at a primal level (almost animalistic) or one I could envision a serial killer might have before he slayed a victim. My alarm meter elevated to the stratosphere. *A glance passed between Janelle and me. A mutual... something was very wrong.*

"I'm calling an ambulance!" I stated emphatically as I turned to get the phone.

"No!" Michael stated in a forceful timbre. "Just let me rest for a bit," he stated in a resigned fashion, suddenly looking and sounding completely spent.

We hurriedly got him dressed, supplied pain medications and piled blankets to warm him. He immediately dozed off. Janelle and I returned upstairs.

"What on earth happened?" I queried.

"I was lying in bed and dad was standing in my doorway. He just kept waving to me and had a strange look on his face. I knew something was off. He was standing there and I could hear the water still running in the shower next door. I jumped out of bed and by the time I saw him again, he was at the couch bending over. He was standing at my bedroom door one second and to the couch the next. He said his back really hurt. That's when I screamed for you," Janelle chronicled objectively.

"Get dressed. We are taking him to the Emergency Room. There is definitely something wrong with him," stating the obvious matter-of-factly.

About an hour later, Michael still would not let us call an ambulance. As happened often in our marriage... *on to game plan B.* I drove our Pilot SUV up a hill on the lawn outside our walkout from the lower level. We wheeled the swivel chair from Michael's downstairs office to the couch and transferred him as gently as possible while battling the unwieldly chair. Once seated, we maneuvered Michael's chair over resistant carpet as far as we could. Again, the adrenaline kicked in and we transported him both awkwardly and painfully for him into the passenger side of the vehicle. I reclined his torso for maximum comfort. Since Michael had sensitive eyes and a mounting headache, I retrieved my ladylike sunglasses from the middle console. I put them on his baby blues and off we drove to the hospital. I felt like Thelma and Louise fleeing our routine lives.

On the way to the emergency room, Michael told his story in short bursts in between spasms of pain.

"I was standing in the shower... I knew I was going to go down...I didn't want to fall, so I eased myself onto the floor of the shower... I am not sure how long I was down, but I can tell you one thing for certain. Hot water does not last long, but cold water lasts forever... I couldn't move... I'm not sure how I got out but somehow crawled out of the shower after I was a human Popsicle... I waved good morning to Janelle and then I was at the couch and you were there. That's all I remember."

My nurse training kicked in and I tried to further assess the situation. Intending to pepper Michael with questions, I didn't get too far.

I said, "Are you sure you didn't fall in the shower, hit your head... anything?"

"No, I knew I was going down. I didn't fall."

I hadn't seen any injuries on him when dressing him earlier so believed his recall of events.

Janelle from the back seat piped in "Are you in a lot of pain dad?"

"Scale one to ten how bad is it?" I added on.

"Twelve." Michael stated.

"Why didn't you call for help?" Janelle asked. "I was right next door."

"I don't know. I guess I didn't think about it," her dad replied... *another questioning glance passed between mother and daughter via the rear view mirror.*

That was the end of the conversation. I could tell he didn't want to talk so I lifted my finger to my lips indicating to Janelle we should be quiet and let her dad rest.

I felt a nervous pit in my stomach as well as massive relief as we pulled into the Emergency Room parking lot fifteen minutes later.

Michael, who loathed doctors' and hospitals' was about to begin an odyssey dealing with both. As we passed through the automatic Emergency Room door, I reflected on the irony of starting my day working on electronic patient files and how a few hours later my husband will become one of them!

CPSIA information can be obtained
at www.ICGtesting.com
Printed in the USA
BVHW071005121220
595542BV00002B/71

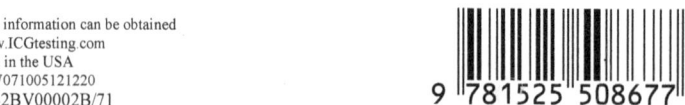

9 781525 508677